*IMAGES of our Past*

# HALIFAX & *the* ROYAL CANADIAN NAVY

## John Boileau

NIMBUS
PUBLISHING

# DEDICATION

To the men and women of the Royal Canadian Navy,
1910–1968, and their successors in Maritime Command
of the Canadian Forces, 1968 to the present. They served their
country faithfully in both war and peace, and most of them
came to know the great port city of Halifax.

Nimbus Publishing Limited
PO Box 9166, Halifax, NS B3K 5M8
(902) 455-4286 nimbus.ca

Printed and bound in Canada
Design: John van der Woude
Author photo: Mark Doucette

Front cover: The Halifax-built Tribal class destroyers
(L-R) *Athabaskan, Nootka, Micmac,* and *Cayuga* in Halifax, July 9, 1962.
Back cover: The first group of recruits from Nova Scotia for HMCS *Niobe*
pose stiffly in their new uniforms, c.1910

Library and Archives Canada Cataloguing in Publication

Boileau, John
Halifax and the Royal Canadian Navy / John Boileau.
(Images of our past) Includes bibliographical
references and index. ISBN 978-1-55109-747-3

1. Halifax (N.S.)—History, Naval. 2. Canada. Royal Canadian Navy—History. 3. Halifax (N.S.)—
History, Naval—Pictorial works. 4. Canada. Royal Canadian Navy—History—Pictorial works. I. Title.
II. Series: Images of our past

FC231.B63 2010 971.6'22 C2009-907276-9

We acknowledge the financial support of the Government of Canada through
the Book Publishing Industry Development Program (BPIDP) and the Canada Council,
and of the Province of Nova Scotia through the Department of Tourism, Culture
and Heritage for our publishing activities.

# CONTENTS

# ACKNOWLEDGEMENTS

THE RESEARCH AND WRITING OF THIS BOOK have been a distinct pleasure for me as they reminded me of my sea cadet days ashore and afloat. Although I spent thirty-seven years in the army, my introduction to military life was in the navy. During my first year of high school, I joined Royal Canadian Sea Cadet Corps Moncton at a time when the navy was still wearing the traditional "square rig" of blue V-neck jumper with white gunshirt, square collar, black silk, and white lanyard, worn with bell-bottomed trousers and a flat white cap with a black tally band. When participating as a member of the corps's drill team, I also wore white accoutrements consisting of gaiters and a web belt. By the time I left cadets three years later, I had risen to the dizzying height of Leading Cadet, proudly displaying an anchor and two chevrons on my left arm. Sadly, almost alone among the world's navies, the Canadian Navy no longer wears its traditional and distinctive uniform.

No work of historical non-fiction is written in isolation, and I would like to thank several people who helped put this book together, either directly or indirectly. I must first acknowledge the fine work of the many naval authors who are listed in the bibliography, and whose earlier research contributed materially to this book. As well, the assistance provided by Marilyn Gurney and Rick Sanderson at the Maritime Command Museum, Christine Duffy at the Shearwater Aviation Museum, the staff at Nova Scotia Archives and Records Management, John Clevett of Formation Imaging Services at Maritime Forces Atlantic, and Commander Richard Oland at HMCS *Scotian* in locating images was invaluable. The helpful research done by Jeanne Howell at the Cambridge Military Library was also instrumental in writing this book, as was the kindness of my neighbour, Commodore Mike Cooper, in letting me make frequent use of his naval library. I must also thank Mike and Captain Bryan Elson for reading the draft manuscript for me with naval eyes and for their advice on naval terminology.

Once again, the top-notch team at Nimbus gets full marks for their assistance, their skills, and for just being such nice people with whom to work. In particular, I must thank general manager Dan Soucoup and senior editor Patrick Murphy for so readily agreeing to my idea for this book. Additionally, the sterling work of editor Paula Sarson made my words read so much better. The interpretation of events, of course, remains strictly my own.

And, as always, thanks to Miriam.

JBB
"Lindisfarne"
Glen Margaret, Nova Scotia
January 12, 2010
*One hundredth anniversary of the introduction of the Naval Service Act*
*into the House of Commons*

## NOTE
# NAVAL NOMENCLATURE FOR THE NOVICE

MOST PROFESSIONS USE TERMINOLOGY unique to their members, whether bricklayers or neurosurgeons. It was no different for sailors of the Royal Canadian Navy (RCN), and their terms reflected a rich tradition stretching back centuries. It was often a bewildering experience for those new to the sea and to ships, whose daily routines were suddenly governed by a complicated system of bells and watches, none of which seemed initially to make any sense.

Canadian warships were (and still are) referred to as HMCS *Halifax*, or the *Halifax*, or simply *Halifax*. They were never referred to as the HMCS *Halifax* (i.e., the Her Majesty's...). Sailors worked and lived "in" ships, never "on" them. Much to the chagrin of today's politically correct crowd who attempt to neuter our rich vocabulary, Canadian sailors and those who followed the sea happily referred to ships as "she" and "her" and never thought they might possibly be offending anyone.

Once on board, new sailors learned that nearly every object had a new name, whether common items or those unique to their ship. Sailors walked on decks with deckheads above, and were surrounded by bulkheads. Some bulkheads had scuttles to see outside. Sailors traversed a ship along flats, while to go from one deck to another they used ladders. Toilets were the heads.

When sailors were hungry, they ate their meals—which were prepared in a galley—in a mess particular to their trade. This was known as broadside messing and continued until the mid-1950s, when all new ship construction featured cafeteria-style meal service. Sailors also slept in their mess, in hammocks slung above the tables, until the introduction of cafeteria messing. They kept small personal belongings, such as needles and threads, letters, combs, and razors stowed nearby in a ditty box. For officers, their mess was called a wardroom, and they had the added luxury of some privacy in a cabin; although, except for the captain, it was usually shared with one or two others. When sailors were ill or injured, they went to sick bay (and if they spent too much time there, were referred to as sick bay rangers).

*Doing laundry at sea was a labour-intensive task, a process known as "dhobbying"— a term inherited from the British in India. Ratings Sandy Donaldson and Norm Gasse dhobbying aboard* HMCS Saguenay, *October 30, 1941.*

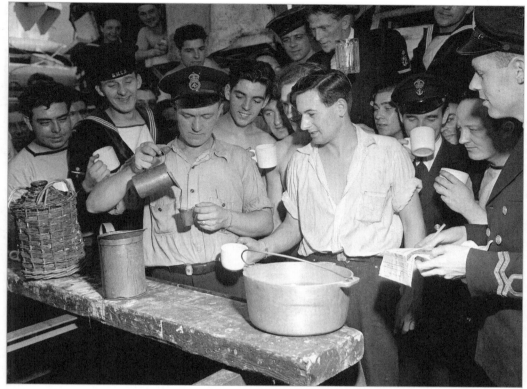

*Sailors aboard* HMCS Arvida *eagerly await an extra tot of their daily grog to celebrate the news of the surrender of Italy, September 8, 1943.*

Sailors, whose junior members were known as ratings or hands, were part of a ship's company. Any items the navy issued to them were pusser, and they were expected to keep them, as well as their working and living areas, tiddley—clean, neat, and smart. This included dhobbying their clothes using a bucket and scrub brush during periods of make and mend.

Throughout its history, the Royal Canadian Navy continued the venerable Royal Navy tradition of a daily ration of a tot (one-eighth of a pint) of rum mixed with two parts water to make grog. Once a ship's bosun's mate sounded "Up Spirits" on his pipe, all sailors over twenty years of age gathered to be issued their tot, usually by a victualling storesman, supervised by a supply branch petty officer and the officer of the day. Teetotallers were marked in the ship's books with a "T" for temperance and drew a small allowance in lieu of grog. On rare occasions, an order would be received to splice the main brace, which meant a double tot for the entire crew for a job well done or to mark a special event.

Sailors were treated to a nightly cup of kye, and the steaming hot chocolate did wonders for the morale, especially during the heavy weather often encountered in the North

Atlantic. When in port, sailors who were authorized to go ashore took the liberty boat—even if it entailed simply walking down the brow (gangway). Once in port—at home or away—sailors who got into trouble might be apprehended by the shore patrol and find themselves as defaulters undergoing a disciplinary hearing at the captain's table, where a suitable punishment would be meted out. Naval terminology was so ingrained in many sailors that they continued to use it ashore in non-naval settings, often to the confusion of the uninitiated.

# THE NAVY TURNS ONE HUNDRED

ON MAY 4, 1910, THE LIBERAL GOVERNMENT of Sir Wilfrid Laurier proclaimed the Naval Service Act, which created the Royal Canadian Navy. Its first ships were two decrepit, hand-me-down British cruisers, His (Her during the reign of a queen) Majesty's Canadian Ship (HMCS) *Niobe* and HMCS *Rainbow*. *Niobe* was stationed on the East Coast, at Halifax—Canada's principal naval port—while *Rainbow* was on the West Coast, at Esquimalt. When the First World War started four years later, the RCN had 379 officers and men. By the end of the war, its strength had risen to more than 100 warships and approximately 9,600 personnel. Throughout the war, the navy remained essentially a coastal patrol force.

During the interwar years, the RCN almost ceased to exist, torpedoed by politicians who were intent on saving money. Its early postwar ships continued to be British castoffs,

*The first group recruits from Nova Scotia for HMCS* Niobe *pose stiffly in their new uniforms, c.1910.*

and it was not until 1931 that the navy acquired its first vessels built expressly for Canada, HMC Ships *Skeena* and *Saguenay*. To keep the navy alive between the wars, its leaders took a page from the army's book and established naval reserve units in major cities across the country—just as the army had done so successfully with the militia. If Canadians would not go to the navy, the navy would come to them. The creation of these naval reserve divisions was at once a stroke of genius and one of the most important measures in preparing the RCN for the Second World War.

At the beginning of that war, the RCN had thirty-eight hundred sailors, six destroyers, and a handful of smaller ships. During the war, its sailors and ships fought around the globe, although of necessity their main arenas were the North Atlantic and the Gulf of St. Lawrence. The RCN played a key role in the longest campaign of the war, the Battle of the Atlantic, with Halifax as one of its major centres of operations. RCN vessels escorted more than twenty-five thousand merchant ships carrying more than 180,000,000 tons of essential supplies to Europe. The RCN lost two thousand sailors and thirty-three ships during the war, nineteen of them due to enemy action. It sank thirty-three submarines on its own or in co-operation with other ships and planes, and destroyed eleven enemy surface ships. Within six years, the navy had become (briefly) the third-largest navy in the

*HMCS Saguenay—one of the RCN's first purpose-built warships—enters Halifax Harbour on arrival from Britain, July 31, 1931.*

*Standing on the quarterdeck by the depth charge throwers, a Canadian sailor keeps watch over merchant ships sailing in a convoy somewhere in the North Atlantic during the Second World War.*

world—more than one hundred thousand uniformed men and women and nine hundred vessels, including more than four hundred warships.

After the Second World War, the RCN went through a brief period of decline before the twin realities of the Cold War and the Korean Conflict led the government to initiate a shipbuilding programme unprecedented outside of war, as well as the creation of a naval aviation branch. In many ways, the 1950s marked the zenith of the navy in peacetime. The St. Laurent-class destroyers were built—described by many as the Cadillacs of destroyers; aircraft carriers were acquired with a range of aircraft, including Banshee jets, to fly off them; the use of helicopters from warships—a Canadian development—was refined; a submarine service was created; and the navy's only icebreaker, HMCS *Labrador*, and the world's fastest warship, the hydrofoil HMCS *Bras d'Or*, were designed, constructed, and launched in Canada.

This period of expansion was followed by another reversal of fortunes, which began in 1968 with the integration and unification of the Royal Canadian Navy, the Canadian Army, and the Royal Canadian Air Force (RCAF) into the Canadian Forces (CF). Although

*HMCS* St. Laurent *was the lead ship of the so-called "Cadillac" destroyers, the first warships entirely designed and built in Canada. The ship's badge is shown at lower left and contains a white whale, said to be the protective spirit of the St. Lawrence River.*

this decline eventually slowed and, in some cases has been reversed, many effects are still felt today. This year, as the Canadian Navy—no longer termed the Royal Canadian Navy—enters its second century, there are several reasons to be optimistic about its future, a potential based on the foundations of its first century.

*

This book is not a history of the RCN, nor is it a history of the port city of Halifax and its great harbour. Rather, it is a collection of stories about the navy in Halifax, in both peace and war. The connection between the navy and the city has been a long and normally friendly one. At times, however, it has also been a decidedly rocky relationship, usually the result of the pressures of wartime.

During the First World War, many Haligonians blamed the navy for the disastrous explosion of December 6, 1917, which levelled the city's north end and caused nearly two thousand deaths with several times as many injured. A generation later, the pent-up frustrations of sailors due to their treatment by officials and citizens in Halifax during the Second World War boiled over into the V-E Day riots. Despite these incidents, generally the association between the navy and its principal port has been mutually beneficial.

Three-quarters of our planet is covered by water, and it is those waters that are the true homes of navies. Sailors and ships from Halifax have ventured far from their home

*Sailors and civilians pass shops looted during the V-E Day riots in Halifax on May 7, 1945, one of the blackest eyes ever delivered to any city in Canada.*

port to many far-flung seas and oceans. To carry out their mission of defending Canada, in both war and peace, ships and sailors from Halifax have steamed through the waters of the North Atlantic, the Caribbean, the Arctic, the English Channel and the North Sea, the Mediterranean, the Pacific, the Far East, and elsewhere. Because the chronicles of sailors and ships far from Halifax in distant waters are such an integral part of the navy's story, some of them form an important part of this book's narrative.

*The 1,000-ton Canadian Government Ship* Canada, *pictured in Halifax Harbour in August 1905, was one of the country's first two armed patrol vessels and had been ordered the previous year. She carried four guns and had a speed of twenty-two knots.*

CHAPTER 1

# HUMBLE BEGINNINGS

## THE CANADIAN MARINE SERVICE

IN 1870, WHEN MOST OF THE BRITISH forces left Canada, except for small naval elements and military garrisons at Halifax and Esquimalt, the Canadian government established the short-lived Marine Police to combat poaching by American fishermen in Canadian waters. The force's six schooners were barely in operation when it was disbanded the next year, the result of the Treaty of Washington between Britain and the United States, which was intended to settle all remaining disputes between the two countries.

The Americans unilaterally abrogated the fisheries provisions of the treaty in 1885, forcing Canada to quickly re-establish a Fisheries Protection Service (FPS). Although the Canadian government ratified a new agreement in 1888, the United States Senate refused to sign on, and the FPS became a permanent branch of the federal government. The Royal Navy (RN) was supposed to enforce fisheries agreements with the United States, but Britain simply would not get involved, leaving the responsibility to Canada by default.

At the time, Britain was forced to limit most of its navy to home waters and avoid conflicts elsewhere. This was a result of the Industrial Revolution, which by the late 1800s led to the rise of several new powers, many of which considered navies as one of the best ways to project an image of strength. In 1902, Britain signed a treaty with Japan, effectively leaving the defence of the western hemisphere to a rapidly growing United States Navy (USN). That same year, Prime Minister Sir Wilfrid Laurier announced that Canada would develop a navy for local protection, under the aegis of the Department of Marine and Fisheries, by the militarization of the FPS.

In 1904, Canada ordered its first armed patrol vessels—*Canada* and *Vigilant*—two modern, high-speed, steel-hulled cruisers, mounting quick-firing guns. Concurrently, Raymond Préfontaine, the minister of Marine and Fisheries, drafted a bill to create a naval

*The ship's company of the Royal Navy Apollo class cruiser HMS* Indefatigable *poses on deck in Halifax Harbour shortly before the British departure in 1905. Halifax was a major station for the Royal Navy for more than 150 years.*

militia, which would train on the new vessels, and a naval academy. When the minister died suddenly in 1905, his bill died with him. The new minister, Louis-Philippe Brodeur, intended to continue the militarization of the FPS, while planning for a new and larger service. But at the time, Laurier and his government were more concerned with the final departure of the Royal Navy and British Army from Halifax and Esquimalt and the subsequent takeover of the extensive facilities they left behind.

In 1905–1906, the last of the RN ships and British Army units left Canada. Their exodus marked the conclusion of a story that stretched back more than three centuries in North America. In the port city, the British left behind them vast and valuable buildings, facilities, and land, among them the dockyard, the Citadel, Royal Artillery Park, and Wellington Barracks (the future *Stadacona*), as well as several forts and batteries, all of which were turned over to the Dominion government. Canada then became responsible for a larger share of its defence, an expense that the new country had largely been able to avoid previously. Without its own navy, Canada had no need for the dockyard but agreed to maintain it for Britain in case of an emergency.

## THE CREATION OF THE NAVY

THE IDEAS OF LAURIER AND BRODEUR changed suddenly when an announcement was made in the British House of Commons in March 1909 that the German fleet would soon outpace Britain's. To generations raised on the concept that "Britannia Rules the Waves," in particular to the many imperialists in Canada and elsewhere in the British Empire, it was a shock to think that the navy of another country might soon outstrip the pre-eminent Royal Navy.

As a result, two resolutions were put forward in the House of Commons, both of which passed unanimously and paved the way for the creation of a Canadian navy. The first one, on March 29, proposed that "in view of her great and varied resources, of her geographical position and natural environments, and of that spirit of self-help and self-respect which alone benefits a strong and growing people, Canada should no longer delay in assuming her proper share of the responsibility and financial burden incident to suitable protection of her exposed coastline and great seaports."

The second one was proposed by Laurier himself. While noting that "the payment of regular and periodic contribution to the imperial treasury for naval and military purposes" was unsatisfactory, Laurier asked the House to "cordially approve of any necessary expenditure designed to promote the speedy organization of a Canadian naval service." At an imperial conference that summer, Britain tried to convince the dominions to participate in the expansion of the RN through direct monetary contributions, but Canada and Australia demurred. The Admiralty's fallback position was that any dominion fleets should be capable of rapid integration into the RN in wartime. For Canada, the appropriate fleet

*Prime Minister Sir Wilfrid Laurier was instrumental in the creation of the Royal Canadian Navy.*

was deemed to be a heavy cruiser, four light cruisers, and six destroyers. It was up to the Laurier government to form such a navy.

The non-partisan co-operation that marked the passage of the two earlier resolutions quickly disappeared and Laurier's plan was attacked from both sides, derided by some as creating a "tin-pot" navy. Many of Robert Borden's opposition Conservatives condemned it for not going far enough; they wanted Canada to fund battleships for the RN. Quebec Liberals screamed even louder, viewing such a fleet as providing the potential for Canada to be dragged into Britain's international affairs, concerns that were clearly not Canada's.

Despite the opposition to his plan, on January 10, 1910, Laurier introduced his Naval Service Act in the House. It proposed a fleet of eleven Canadian-built warships—five cruisers and six destroyers—for use in local waters, maintained by an annual expenditure of three million dollars. During the debates that followed the introduction of the act, Laurier uttered his famous statement in response to a suggestion from Borden that a Canadian navy could stand by if Britain were attacked: "If England is at war we are at war and liable to attack."

The vote on the bill on March 10 was split along party lines—111 to 70, with 18 abstentions. On May 4, 1910, the Naval Service of Canada was created, and Britain formally transferred the naval dockyard to Canada, requiring Canada to let the RN use it when necessary. Canada now had a navy, but it existed only on paper. Before Laurier could do anything about making the navy a real force, his government was defeated in the general election of 1911, partly due to the naval issue. His successor, Borden, who favoured direct financial support to the RN, was blocked in his efforts by the Liberal-controlled Senate. The net result was that when the First World War broke out three years later, there was neither a proper Canadian navy in existence nor any British warships financed by Canada.

*Rear Admiral Charles Kingsmill, first director of the Canadian Naval Service, c.1910.*

ON THE MORNING OF October 22, 1910, the aging, ex-RN (some said discarded), 11,000-ton Diadem class lightly armoured cruiser HMCS *Niobe* steamed into Halifax Harbour, escorted by the Canadian Government Ships *Canada* and *Minto*. Flag and bunting bedecked—"dressed" in nautical terms—she fired her guns in salute of her new home port, as Citadel cannons echoed a welcome. Rear Admiral Charles Kingsmill, a Canadian who had served in the RN and became the first director of the Canadian Naval Service, went aboard and hoisted his pennant, the first time a Canadian flag officer did so in a major warship.

Commissioned in 1898, the long-obsolescent *Niobe* was 132 metres long and could make 20.5 knots. She carried sixteen 6-inch guns, twelve 12-pounders, five 3-pounders, five 2-pounders, and two 18-inch torpedo tubes. Her wartime complement was seven hundred sailors. The entire strength of the RCN at the time was 350 officers and men. These shortcomings did not deter officials from making grand rhetorical statements so typical of the time. Minister Brodeur proclaimed the cruiser's arrival as "a dawning epoch of self-reliance," in which *Niobe* would "plant the standard of progress and true Canadian national greatness upon the virgin slopes of a glorious future that unrolls its splendid proportions before our vision today."

Others were less kind. The *Bridgewater Bulletin* termed *Niobe*'s arrival as merely an occasion for Haligonians to pompously "throw out their chests and strut around in gay uniforms." This "expensive toy" would do little more than provide an opportunity for government graft, at the same time training politicians' sons "to wear natty uniforms at five o'clock teas."

To make up crew shortfalls, Britain loaned Canada six hundred RN sailors for a two-year term, who would operate *Niobe* (and her sister ship *Rainbow* on the West Coast),

*Exercising a gun crew aboard* HMCS *Niobe, c.1911. The lieutenant controlling the practice has adopted a convenient position for observing the fall of shot and directing the crew. The sailors are wearing No. 3 dress. The tapes securing the right-hand breech worker's trousers have come undone and are hanging down.*

while Canadians were recruited and trained. *Niobe*'s career in Canadian service almost came to a premature end when she went aground off Cape Sable on the night of July 30–31, 1911, and was nearly lost. It took more than a year before the necessary repairs were completed at the end of 1912.

## ROYAL NAVAL COLLEGE OF CANADA

ABOUT THE ONLY GOOD THING to happen once the government created the navy was the establishment of the Royal Naval College of Canada (RNCC) in Halifax. The college occupied the old naval hospital at the extreme north end of the dockyard, a long, narrow, four-storey, red brick building built in the 1860s. When the RN departed, the hospital had closed and its contents were sold at public auction. The new college was established to train prospective officers in naval science, tactics, and strategy. The college opened its doors in January 1911 with a class of twenty-one cadets. The commandant and uniformed instructional staff were supplied by the Admiralty, supplemented by three civilian school-masters who taught mathematics, science, and languages.

Commander Edward Nixon became commandant in 1915, termed a "wonderful man" by many of his charges. In Hal Lawrence's *Tales of the North Atlantic,* Cadet Alured

TOP *The building that housed the Royal Naval College of Canada, photographed on July 23, 1926. The college opened in 1911 in the old naval hospital in HMC Dockyard, Halifax.*

BOTTOM *Cadets of the Royal Naval College of Canada pose on the front steps of the college shortly before the outbreak of the First World War in 1914. L–R: A. R. Pressey, R. Oland, O. Critchley, R. M. Puddescombe, V. S. Godfrey, F. L. Houghton, E. Sherwood, G. M. Hibbard. Oland was in charge of the Naval Control Service at Halifax when the Second World War started in 1939 (chapter 4).*

Musgrave recalled how Nixon handled defaulters. "We learned not to give long contrived stories as to why we had erred." Nixon would simply ask "Why?" until the story got shorter and shorter and even the cadets realized how silly their explanations were. "We learned it was best to say 'guilty'; we were, usually, and it saved time." For punishment, Nixon would usually stop their pocket money or award extra drill.

Cadet John Grant, a member of the first class, told Lawrence "We didn't have many facilities. No rugby ground, no cricket field, but we played grass hockey on the hard ground of the dockyard." The academic side was traditional but had "a tremendous amount of practical engineering," as Grant recalled. On successful completion of a two-year course (almost immediately increased to three years), cadets went to Britain to get their "big ship time" in an RN cruiser.

## THE FIRST CASUALTIES

THE OUTBREAK OF THE First World War in August 1914 put Halifax back into the role it had played so many times before. Because of Canada's status at the time—so clearly enunciated earlier by Laurier—when Britain was at war, Canada was automatically at war. Canadians responded patriotically to the call to arms. Although the First Canadian Contingent sailed from Quebec in October 1914, all other troops departed from Halifax—nearly 285,000 before the war ended in 1918.

Warships and merchant vessels were constantly leaving and departing the harbour, while formidable defences on its shores and islands bristled with coastal artillery, machine guns, and searchlights. Two steel-mesh submarine nets stretched across its entrance. Allied and neutral ships entered through a narrow gap in it that was opened and closed by gate vessels, while minesweepers patrolled the outer approaches to make sure that enemy submarines had not laid any mines. Halifax quickly became one of the busiest ports in the world, handling 15,000,000 tons annually—more than 700 per cent over pre-war tonnages.

Surprisingly, Canada's first casualties of the First World War were not soldiers but four young midshipmen. On August 14, 1914, just ten days after the start of the war, the RN armoured cruiser HMS *Good Hope* arrived in Halifax to take on coal and left the next day. She was part of a squadron of two old heavy cruisers, a light cruiser, and a converted merchant ship auxiliary cruiser that would be dispatched to the Pacific in search of the German Asiatic Squadron under Admiral Graf von Spee, whose two heavy and three light cruisers were a threat to shipping in the Pacific.

When the squadron sailed, it carried four recent graduates from the Royal Naval College of Canada to help make up crew shortfalls. In Halifax, Rear Admiral Sir Christopher Cradock, commanding the force, had shifted his flag to *Good Hope*. He specifically requested Midshipmen Arthur Silver of Halifax, the chief cadet captain, and William

*The Royal Navy armoured cruiser* HMS *Good Hope, flying the flag of Rear Admiral Sir Christopher Cradock from its mainmast, in Halifax Harbour in the fall of 1914 before she departed on her final, fateful cruise.*

Palmer, also from Halifax, and the senior midshipman, join the ship's gun room. Two other midshipmen, Malcolm Cann from Yarmouth and Victor Hathaway from Fredericton, were selected by lot. They all left Halifax in *Suffolk* and transferred to *Good Hope* at sea off New York. All four had entered the college in 1911.

Classmate John Grant remembered Hathaway as "very fine looking, modest, very nice, played the piano for our singsongs, a promising young officer," while Palmer was "very brainy, used to be top of the class apparently without having to work." Grant described Silver as "rather like Hathaway, very well-known Halifax family, keen fisherman and famous for his art in casting" and thought Cann was "a good mess mate."

On November 1, the British Squadron was patrolling off Coronel, Chile, when it encountered the German flotilla. Outmatched, outgunned, and outranged, Cradock and his sailors bravely faced the enemy. In the hour-long gunnery duel that followed, *Monmouth* was sunk and *Good Hope* was reduced to a flaming hulk. She blew up and sank with most of her crew, including the four Canadian "middies." It was a major blow to the future senior leadership of the RCN.

## THE FIRST WORLD WAR

PRIME MINISTER ROBERT BORDEN, a lawyer from the Annapolis Valley town of Grand Pré, cabled London in the fall of 1914 asking what course of action Canada should take if his government decided to offer naval aid. The reply in October was less than encouraging: "Admiralty inform don't think anything effectual can now be done as ships take too long to build and advise Canadian assistance be concentrated on army."

*Prime Minister Sir Robert Borden, Canada's remarkable leader during the First World War, c.1915.*

Due to government inaction and procrastination since its formation four years earlier, the RCN was totally unprepared to fight a war at sea when the First World War broke out. *Niobe* kept breaking down during coastal patrols, and subsequently spent most of her days alongside at Halifax, undergoing maintenance and repairs. In any case, there were only 350 trained sailors to man her or any other warships. When the war started, Canada turned operational control of *Niobe* over to the RN. Reacting to the demands of war, she was ready to go to sea in three weeks. Extra sailors had been rushed from the West Coast to man her, the crews of two old sloops no longer fit to fight. Additional manpower came from across the country in the form of volunteers with various kinds of experience, as well as 107 trained seamen from the Royal Naval Reserve in St. John's, Newfoundland, which brought *Niobe* to her full complement of 700 for the first time since becoming a Canadian warship.

With RN Captain Robert Corbett in command, *Niobe*'s first wartime task was to escort a troopship carrying the Royal Canadian Regiment—the country's only regular infantry unit—from its garrison at Halifax to Bermuda in September. Because of various defects, *Niobe* was denied the opportunity of escorting the First Canadian Contingent when it sailed from Quebec City at the end of October, a great thirty-ship armada of troopships carrying thirty thousand soldiers protected by RN warships. Instead, she searched off the Strait of Belle Isle, looking for a suspected German surface raider that had been erroneously reported in the Gulf of St. Lawrence.

Meanwhile, Prime Minister Borden made his case to Britain again in November, pressing for destroyers and submarines to be built in Canada and for the RN to lend the RCN ships until they were completed. Winston Churchill, Britain's First Sea Lord, repeated the earlier message: the RN had no ships to spare and building ships in Canada was impractical; instead soldiers were needed from the Dominion. The results of shelving Laurier's shipbuilding plans had come home to roost.

As the RCN cast about for suitable ships, a few patriotic—and rich—Canadians helped

*Sunday church service aboard* HMCS Niobe *as she helps enforce the blockade off New York, 1914. A merchant vessel sails by in the background.*

out. Flamboyant Montreal millionaire yachtsman Jack Ross, medically rejected by the army, turned to the navy with an offer it could not refuse. He had already donated his small yacht *Albacore*—suitable only for harbour work—and now offered another one, providing he got to command it. Ross went to New York and purchased Willie K. Vanderbilt's twenty-four-knot yacht *Tarantula*, reputedly one of the first high-speed steam-turbine ships. Rechristened HMCS *Tuna* at Halifax, at Ross's expense she was fitted out with a 3-pounder gun and two torpedo tubes and entered service in December 1914.

In the fall of 1914, *Niobe* joined the RN's Bermuda-based 4th Cruiser Squadron blockading thirty-two German merchant ships sheltering in neutral New York Harbour. The work was tedious and boring: stopping, boarding, and searching every vessel for contraband intended for Germany or for German nationals trying to get back home to help the war effort. After sixteen days on station, it was back to Halifax for the dirty, dusty task of coaling ship, taking on fresh provisions, and then returning to duty.

Already decrepit, *Niobe* was soon worn out by her blockading duties. By July 1915, her funnels were collapsing, while her boilers and main bulkheads were in poor condition. A major refit was necessary, but *Niobe* was too old to make it worthwhile. She returned to

Halifax and never put to sea again. Instead, she was paid off in September and became a depot ship. Although the Admiralty offered a replacement newer by three years, the RCN simply did not have the sailors to man her. By now, the navy was largely involved in another role: coastal patrol and protection of shipping.

## HALIFAX

DESPITE ITS EXCELLENT LOCATION for conducting defence of trade operations in the North Atlantic, Halifax was ill-prepared to carry them out. Its dockyard facilities and staff were in old and cramped buildings, the result of the government's vacillating and inconsistent attitude towards the development of the RCN since its creation in 1910. Rear Admiral R. S. Phipps Hornby, commander-in-chief North America and West Indies Station, reported in June 1915 that the facilities could only meet the requirements of fishery protection vessels and had no modern machinery.

Phipps Hornby noted the dockyard could only carry out minor repairs on warships; larger work would have to be done by the Halifax Graving Dock Company, a commercial operation, which specialized in merchant ships and did not "necessarily give priority to naval work and their charges are extremely high." Facilities at the RN's dockyard in

*Rear Admiral R. S. Phipps Hornby (seated centre, with beard), RN commander-in-chief at Halifax, poses with his officers aboard the Cunard liner* Caronia, *which was requisitioned by the British government in 1914 as an armed merchant cruiser.*

*In 1914, the Halifax waterfront was a rabbit warren of rundown wooden buildings.*

Bermuda were superior. Yet, he selected Halifax as the main base for his ships, due to its location, ease of entering its harbour, and communications facilities.

After the First Canadian Contingent sailed from Quebec to Britain in October 1914, all subsequent troopships departed from Halifax. The presence of thousands of soldiers— if only temporarily—as well as thousands of British and Canadian sailors and merchant seamen, overwhelmed local authorities and concerned citizens. There were simply too many servicemen to be looked after during their off-duty hours by too few citizens willing to invite them into their homes. Coupled with a lack of entertainment facilities—a large recreation hut erected by the YMCA opposite Government House on Barrington Street was about all that existed—there was little opportunity for service personnel to relax. And then the provincial government compounded the problem by closing all city bars.

Prior to the war, Halifax had been exempt from various federal and provincial statutes outlawing alcohol. During the war, the same small minds that had agitated for the Temperance Acts pressured the provincial authorities to rescind Halifax's exemptions. The reformers succeeded, and on July 1, 1916, every bar in the city closed. Now servicemen had no place to even buy a beer. Amazingly, the outcry against the new law was not based on the fact that it deprived sailors and soldiers of a well-earned drink, but that it would deprive liquor wholesalers and retailers of their business and throw their employees out of work.

As it would be again during the Second World War, the government action was a mistake. Drinking establishments simply went underground, where they were known as "blind pigs," offering spirits of questionable provenance and quality. These surreptitious drinking holes were usually connected to another off-duty pastime frequently associated with sailors—brothels. Like any port city, Halifax had always had its share of prostitutes, but before the war they were generally confined to streetwalkers and to small, dingy establishments which operated behind drawn blinds along Water Street and in the shadow of Citadel Hill.

In his popular history of the city, *Halifax: Warden of the North*, Thomas H. Raddall described what happened next:

> "*The local drabs were not enough for this male swarm. Into the city poured a stream of eager prostitutes from every part of Canada, but especially from Montreal. These professionals set themselves up, in squads of three or four, in small "cigarette shops"—they had a stock of honest tobacco and matches, but the windows were obscured by large cardboard cigarette advertisements, and there were always two or three narrow inner dens furnished with a red lamp, a couch, and a bowl of disinfectant. These opened for business in the old naughty quarters, but soon appeared along the northern ends of Gottingen and Barrington streets towards the old north railway station and about the dockyard and the sidings where the troop trains lay.*"

## THE U-BOAT THREAT

THE REASON FOR THE RCN's change of mission to coastal patrol and shipping protection was German submarines, or *unterseebooten*, hence U-boats. The German U-boat war began in earnest on February 1, 1915, against merchant vessels, including neutrals, in British home waters, with the aim of starving Britain into submission. This action met with considerable success at first, as few effective anti-submarine weapons had yet been developed. The number of sinkings rose dramatically and by the summer of 1915 had reached almost one hundred a month. Despite these losses, the Admiralty still did not initiate the convoy system—a time-proven method of reducing shipping losses—for merchant ships, which continued to sail independently. The only ships that received escorts were troopships.

The political cost to Germany was great. When *U-20* torpedoed the Cunard liner *Lusitania* within sight of the Irish coast in broad daylight on May 7, 1915, there was universal condemnation. Later that month, British officials warned Canada that German U-boats might be expected shortly in the northwest Atlantic. This was followed in June with the suggestion that Canada should establish coastal patrols with small craft obtained locally and "rapidly increase" this patrol service to deal with any submarines that might reach Canadian waters. But how could the tiny, underfunded RCN possibly accomplish such a major task?

*The Royal Canadian Navy commissioned several drifters during the First World War. These small ships were within the capabilities of Canadian shipyards to build.*

## CHAPTER 2

# THE HALIFAX PATROLS

### THE TIN-POT NAVY

Admiral Charles Kingsmill's resources to deal with the U-boat threat were practically non-existent. While a parsimonious government dithered over the expense of purchasing suitable ships, the acquisition of additional private yachts provided some short-term relief. Toronto millionaire John Craig Eaton sold his family yacht, *Florence*, to the government for one dollar, an offer that had initially been rebuffed in August 1914. Commissioned under the same name, she was the only Canadian yacht to join the RCN. Three more American yachts followed, commissioned as HMC Ships *Grilse*, *Hochelaga*, and *Stadacona*. Armed with torpedo tubes and 3- and 6-pounder guns, along with the occasional 12-pounder, they remained among the most useful of the navy's patrol craft until the end of the war.

By September 1915, the RCN had three commissioned vessels, augmented by nine smaller auxiliaries, available for patrols along the coasts of Nova Scotia and the defence of Halifax—where an anti-submarine net now stretched across the harbour entrance—while the remaining commissioned ships were assigned to the Gulf of St. Lawrence patrol. Germany suddenly discontinued its unrestricted U-boat campaign on September 1, 1915. Yet, in only eight months German submarines had sunk nearly 1,000,000 tons of Allied shipping. U-boats had proven themselves as a significant weapon of war; Germany would use them again.

After initially discouraging all Canadian offers for naval ships, in November 1916 the Admiralty advised the RCN to increase its East Coast patrol force to thirty-six ships mounting 12-pounder guns. It also stated that it could do nothing more than provide an officer to advise or take command. Angered, the government responded by noting that Britain had said the Canadian war effort should be based on soldiers and had blocked all proposals by Canada to build warships in the Dominion. Additionally, the RCN had sent every spare gun and volunteer it could find to the RN, with little to show in return.

Kingsmill promptly ordered a dozen trawler-type minesweepers from Canadian Vickers in Montreal (which had assembled ten submarines for the USN the previous year) and Polson Iron Works in Toronto. The Admiralty ordered another two dozen, sent some trained sailors to Canada—including a few Canadians in RN service—and provided a commander for the East Coast patrols, Vice Admiral Sir Charles Coke.

Coke proved to be the worst possible choice for the job and was quickly relieved after alienating officials in both Halifax and Ottawa. While his replacement was on the way, Kingsmill uncharacteristically stepped in and appointed another Canadian, Acting Captain Walter Hose, to the job. Because of the various RN and RCN authorities involved and their sometimes convoluted chains of reporting and command, Hose had a difficult task ahead of him.

Ocean convoys were the responsibility of an RN rear admiral in Sydney, who reported to London, while coastal convoys and other shipping came under the RCN, which reported to Ottawa. Hose was responsible for providing escorts for all of them, including the initial seaward leg of the ocean convoys. Hose's deputy in Halifax, Commander Edward Newcombe, was in charge of the coastal escort ships stationed there. Another player was Rear Admiral William Storey, a retired RN officer, who was superintendent of the dockyard and reported to Ottawa. As such, he had charge of all local defences, including minesweeping and patrols in his area. The top naval officer in the region was Vice Admiral Sir George Patey, the RN's new commander-in-chief North America and West Indies Station, who co-ordinated all British and Canadian authorities in Canada and the United States involved in the protection of shipping.

Kingsmill was often left out in the cold, as the RN continued to regard the RCN as a mere accessory. He had additional problems. His staff was small and inexperienced in the intricacies of proper staff work (as was he; his time had been spent at sea). But his biggest problem was the war on the Western Front, which overshadowed everything he tried to do and completely captured the attention of the politicians.

## THE CONVOY SYSTEM

BY 1917, THE GERMAN HIGH COMMAND considered it essential to start another U-boat campaign and, on February 1, Germany proclaimed unrestricted U-boat warfare against all ships found in British waters or bound for Britain. Allied shipping losses mounted rapidly. In response, the British instituted a number of defensive measures: improvements in anti-submarine warfare such as hydrophones, depth charges, extended minefields, and searchlights. They also finally—and reluctantly—agreed to implement a comprehensive convoy system, despite the desires of the admirals to engage in dramatic fleet actions on the high seas. But it made little sense to "keep the sea lanes open" in the vast empty spaces of the North Atlantic, when it was merchant shipping and troopships that needed protection. Throughout history, convoys had proven their value while independently sailed freighters suffered huge losses.

*Trawlers and drifters of the East Coast patrols underway in Halifax Harbour during the First World War. Built in Canada to Admiralty designs for the RN and RCN, they served in many parts of the world, some surviving into the Second World War.*

Halifax, along with Sydney, became an assembly port for eastbound convoys. The convoys were marshalled and escorted to sea by the RCN, then handed over to the big cruisers of the RN and USN, which acted as ocean escorts. On arrival in British home waters, destroyers and land-based aircraft met them and took them into port. Sinkings decreased dramatically. Convoys from Halifax to Britain—designated HX (Homeward from Halifax)—began on August 21 and included all ships capable of making 12½ knots or more. Once the St. Lawrence River froze, slow convoys also departed from Halifax, putting an even greater strain on already overburdened port facilities—and on the Halifax patrol flotilla.

The success of the convoy system led British naval authorities to believe that German U-boats would cross the Atlantic in search of easier targets, perhaps any time after March 1918. They warned Kingsmill, although he could do little to help. Aircraft were required, but the government of Prime Minister Robert Borden was not prepared to provide the necessary funding. As a stopgap measure, the Admiralty ordered thirty-six trawlers and another hundred drifters from Canadian boatyards. Some would be available as early as spring 1918, but Canadian crews would have to man them.

## THE NAVY AND THE HALIFAX EXPLOSION

AT 9:05 A.M. ON A COLD, clear December 6, 1917, the reality of the First World War was brought home to Halifax. Twenty minutes earlier, the Norwegian ship *Imo* and the French munitions freighter *Mont Blanc* collided in the narrowest part of Halifax Harbour. Steel grating on steel caused sparks, igniting benzol stored on *Mont Blanc*'s deck, which seeped into the holds where 2,766 tons of picric acid, TNT, and guncotton were crammed together. *Imo* drifted towards Dartmouth, while *Mont Blanc*, engulfed in flames, drifted towards Richmond's wooden Pier 6.

When *Mont Blanc*'s volatile mixture exploded, it blew her sixteen hundred metres high and literally shredded the ship, while *Imo* was blown onto the Dartmouth shore. It was the largest man-made, non-nuclear explosion the world has ever seen. The destruction was immense. The blast destroyed everything within eight hundred metres—including the massive Richmond sugar refinery and the dry dock—and damaged buildings within sixteen hundred metres—including several port facilities. Across the harbour at Turtle Grove, the Halifax Breweries and the nearby Mi'kmaq village were totally destroyed.

Within seconds, out of a population of less than fifty thousand, almost two thousand people were dead, nine thousand injured—many from flying bits of metal and glass—and twenty-six thousand left without adequate shelter. Stoves knocked over by the blast ignited shattered wooden houses. Soon blazes burned all over the city's north end. The next day, one of the worst blizzards in years hit the city, adding to the survivors' misery and hampering rescue efforts. Property damage amounted to thirty-five million dollars.

*The wooden-hulled drifter* CD 74 *tied up alongside dockyard buildings damaged in the explosion.*

Many city residents blamed the fledgling RCN for the Halifax Explosion, believing it had failed to adequately control shipping in the harbour. Yet, at the individual level, several sailors—Canadian and British—performed acts of heroism immediately before and after the devastating explosion. After *Mont Blanc* collided with *Imo*, fire broke out in the French ship. *Niobe*'s captain sent his steam pinnace with six volunteers—Stoker Petty Officer Edward Beard and five seamen—under Acting Bosun Albert Mattison to help the stricken vessel.

At the same time as *Niobe*'s steam pinnace headed for *Mont Blanc*, the captain of the RN cruiser HMS *Highflyer* sent his whaler to see if anything could be done. Commander Tom Triggs took six sailors with him. When Triggs got to *Mont Blanc*, engulfed in thirty metre–high flames, he boarded the tug *Stella Maris* and conferred with her captain. Leaving the crews of the tug and *Niobe*'s pinnace to get a line to the burning ship, Triggs returned to the whaler.

As the whaler was pulling towards *Imo*, about 275 metres away, *Mont Blanc* exploded. The force of the explosion blew *Niobe*'s pinnace and its crew to pieces, while the only person to survive on the whaler was Able Seaman William Becker. He was later found on the Dartmouth shore. These Canadian and British sailors were fully aware of the hazardous

TOP *The explosion damaged the dockyard timber store.*
BOTTOM *Windows were blown out and the roof blown off of this dockyard building, although its brick walls withstood the blast.*

nature of their task. By their devotion to duty, they sacrificed their lives trying to save the lives of others.

The explosion also set on fire the ocean-going tug *Musquash*, which carried ammunition. *Highflyer*'s captain asked another tug to take *Musquash* in tow, but the crew were unwilling to board the disabled vessel. Two British sailors, Leading Seaman Thomas Davis and Able Seaman Robert Stones, volunteered to go aboard *Musquash*, now broken loose from her moorings. They secured a line and the tug towed *Musquash* into the middle of the harbour. Then they went forward, pulled the ammunition—by now badly scorched—away from the flames and threw it overboard. The tender *W. H. Lee* arrived and Davis and Stones broke down doors to allow *Lee*'s fire hoses to put out the fire. The sailors' actions subdued the blaze and prevented further damage and loss of life, as the ammunition could have exploded at any time.

Mattison, Beard, Triggs, Becker, Davis, and Stones received the Albert Medal. The medal—in memory of Prince Albert, Queen Victoria's husband—was awarded to those who, "in saving or endeavouring to save the lives of others from shipwreck or other peril of the sea, endangered their own lives." It was later extended to saving life on land.

While the disaster was unfolding in the harbour, two navy divers from *Niobe* were working underwater off the dockyard pier. Four men manned the hand-operated air pumps,

*Sailors assist two of* HMCS Niobe's *divers as they suit up.*

while another two paid out the divers' line under the watchful eye of Chief Master-at-Arms John Gammon. When *Mont Blanc* blew up, one diver was in the water and the other was descending a ladder. The explosion killed five of the six sailors on the wharf, but both divers and Gammon survived.

The surviving sailor, Able Seaman Walter Critch, realized that he had to get air to the divers immediately. Although the pump was undamaged, the pumphouse roof had collapsed onto it. Critch was unable to clear the fallen roof, so he squeezed in between it and the pump and gave a mighty heave upwards with his shoulders. He moved bits of wreckage off the pump wheels and, with one hand holding up the collapsed roof, started the pump with the other.

The piston slowly began to suck in air. It usually took four men to operate the pump, but somehow Critch managed single-handedly to start a trickle of air going to the divers. At the same time, Gammon rushed to the ladder to get the divers up and their face masks open. For their quick actions, Critch received the Meritorious Service Medal (Naval), while Gammon was made a Member of the Order of the British Empire.

The explosion badly damaged *Niobe*, several naval installations, and the Royal Naval College of Canada. At the College, although the outer walls remained standing, interior walls and ceilings collapsed and windows shattered. Many of the cadets and staff were injured, especially by flying glass. Two cadets each lost the sight of one eye. A few days later, the cadets went home on Christmas leave and reassembled two months later at Kingston's Royal Military College to complete the year. The RNCC opened in Esquimalt in August 1918—never to return to Halifax—and then closed in 1922.

*The explosion devastated Halifax's naval dockyard and badly damaged* HMCS Niobe, *on the right.*

# THE HALIFAX PATROLS

FOR SAILORS POSTED TO *Niobe* for dockyard duties and maintenance, it was a frustrating experience. Long days of cleaning, chipping, and painting were interrupted occasionally by ceremonial functions, usually as guards of honour and to hold the crowds back each time a new draft of soldiers departed for overseas. In *Tin-Pots and Pirate Ships*, authors Michael Hadley and Roger Sarty quote rating A. H. Wickens, who noted that it made their "bellies full of being left behind" and "sat on [their] dignities." As members of the senior service, Wickens was particularly displeased sailors had to present arms with fixed bayonets to the departing soldiers, whom he referred to as "those monkeys." To make matters worse, after each troopship left, the sailors had to march back the three kilometres to the dockyard, during which time they were "the victims of much booing and name calling such as: 'home guards and slackers, when are you going over with the real men?'"

By mid-1918, Captain Walter Hose had a hundred small ships, working out of Halifax, Sydney, and St. John's. They performed the unglamorous but essential tasks of ensuring the harbour approaches were clear of enemy ships and mines, convoy assembly, and the initial stage of convoy escort. The small ships were undermanned and poorly equipped. Hose needed twenty-three hundred sailors to do his job, but he only had fifteen hundred. The return of two hundred Canadian naval reservists from Britain, along with the addition of three hundred Newfoundland reservists and a few RN specialists helped, but still left him a couple of hundred short. The warship side was just as bad. Hose did not have one vessel that mounted a gun that could get within effective range of an enemy submarine before the Canadian ship would—in all likelihood—be sunk. He needed fast ships, like sloops and destroyers, not trawlers. None were available from either the RN or USN, although the Americans did send six sub-chasers and two torpedo boats to Halifax to operate under Canadian control.

## THE U-BOAT THREAT

IN MAY 1918, U-BOATS STARTED arriving in North American waters. After successes off the United States coast, *u-156* moved into Canadian waters. On August 2, she stopped the four-masted schooner *Dornfontein* in the Bay of Fundy and set her afire. Over the next two days, seven more schooners were sunk along the Nova Scotia coast. Halifax was in an uproar. Convoy HC-12 was preparing to sail: seventeen ships carrying 12,500 Canadian and American soldiers. Enemy subs could be waiting to pounce right outside the harbour entrance or have laid minefields in the two hundred kilometres of continental shelf.

Despite the threat, the convoy sailed from Halifax on the afternoon of August 4, led by minesweeping trawlers and sub-chasers, with additional trawlers and drifters as close

UC-97, *a German Type UC III mine-laying submarine, shown alongside at Halifax after the war, May 17, 1919. She had surrendered to American forces on November 22, 1918, and was taken on a victory tour. The arrow points to the torpedo tube.* U-156 *was three times larger than* UC-97.

escort. The close escorts could not keep up with the troopships and gradually fell behind. Luckily, *u-156* was further down the south shore, where she unfortunately sank three fishing schooners. The convoy got out of Canadian waters safely, more by good luck than by good seamanship.

Early on the morning of August 5, the British tanker *Luz Blanca* departed Halifax for Mexico. Her master ignored warnings to wait until dusk to sail and to zigzag. Just before noon, about fifty-five kilometres south of the Sambro Light, a torpedo from *u-156*—on its way to Halifax—found its mark and slammed into her hull. Damaged, the tanker turned about while her crew fought the sub with their 12-pounder. Eventually, the *Luz Blanca* lay dead in the water in flames. Her crew took to the lifeboats and bravely began rowing for the Sambro light, twenty-seven kilometres away.

A nearby steamer witnessed the attack and sent out the alarm. The trawlers and drifters returning from convoy HC-12 got the message and came in response, but ended up in the wrong position and found nothing. The sub-chasers were luckier, and picked up the survivors from the lifeboats five hours after the attack. No trace of *u-156* was found; in fact she had headed south immediately after the attack and was long gone when the would-be rescuers arrived.

*HMCS* Cartier *was built in 1910 for the Department of Marine and Fisheries as a hydrographic survey vessel and taken into naval service as an armed patrol vessel in 1917. She was renamed* HMCS Charney *during the Second World War.*

The British commander-in-chief quickly suspended Halifax as a convoy terminal. Future convoys assembled in Sydney and American ports and met far out to sea. Control of local shipping was tightened. On August 7, Admiral Kingsmill issued a tactical instruction to the Halifax patrol, the first ever. It stated that although the Canadian ships would be outgunned by U-boats, they should press home the attack, fire at the pressure hull, zigzag to avoid being hit, and try to cause some damage. The instruction speculated that the subs were a long way from home and, as their mission was to sink merchant shipping, they would probably submerge to avoid the risk of being damaged. Then they could be attacked with depth charges.

*U-156* returned, this time off Cape Breton. The sub captured the steam trawler *Triumph* near Canso and sent her crew off in a rowboat. The U-boat's captain put a gun and some of his submariners aboard the trawler. The instant mini-raider was well-known on the fishing grounds and approached several schooners with ease, sinking six before the German crew scuttled the trawler when they ran out of coal. Meanwhile, *Triumph's* crew rowed ashore at Canso and raised the alarm.

On August 25, west of Saint Pierre, *U-156* sank another small trawler, followed by the capture of four schooners. As she began to sink them with explosives, a small, four-ship

Canadian flotilla came into view, spread out in a search line at intervals of five to six kilometres. *Cartier* led the group, made up of her sister ship *Hochelaga* and two trawlers. From ten kilometres away, *Hochelaga* spotted two schooners and steamed towards them to warn of the enemy sub in the area. Suddenly, one of the schooners disappeared, leaving the low silhouette of the big U-boat clearly visible.

In reaction, *Hochelaga*'s captain, Lieutenant Robert Legate, immediately ordered full speed ahead, came about, and raced back towards *Cartier*, completely ignoring Kingsmill's direction to press home the attack against all enemy subs. At least the flotilla leader in *Cartier* obeyed his admiral's instructions and ordered all ships to go for the U-boat at full speed, as soon as he read Legate's signal "enemy in sight." By then *u-156* had already submerged. The four warships searched through the wreckage of the schooners, without any luck.

The incident had the potential to add an RCN laurel to the long list of stirring RN actions at sea—a small, outclassed David steaming full speed ahead towards an enemy Goliath, guns blazing. Successful or not, it was the type of one-sided battle on which legends were built and could have earned Legate a Victoria Cross. Instead, he was court-martialled.

Legate was an experienced sailor. He had been on active service since the start of the war, was commissioned in 1915, and held command at sea for nearly two years. Yet, at the moment of truth, his nerve had failed him. He was found guilty of failing to "use his utmost execution to bring his ship into action" and dismissed from the navy. The one chance for the fledgling RCN's moment of glory in the face of the enemy had passed, and it was not to come again in this war.

Meanwhile, *u-156* and her sister submarines continued to cut a swath of destruction off the East Coast of Canada, resulting in six more sinkings in August. On her way home to Germany, *u-156* hit a mine off Scotland and sank. That left only the huge 1,700-ton cargo submarine *Deutschland*, now renamed *u-155*, off Nova Scotia. After laying mine-fields near the Sambro Light and Peggy's Cove, she sank a trawler. For safety, the Quebec convoys were thereafter routed north through the Strait of Belle Isle, although all subsequent convoys from both Quebec and Sydney got through unharmed.

The appearance of U-boats off the coast of Nova Scotia had caused panic across the province. Boats were being sunk within sight of the shore, and the RCN seemed helpless to respond. The press ranted and railed against the navy, but there was little it could do with tiny ships, untrained crews, and its biggest guns shipped to Britain for the RN. There were only eleven naval vessels in commission on the entire Canadian East Coast, and only five of them could put to sea, with the remaining six restricted to operations close inshore.

Naval department officials scrambled to find additional ships. They called up a postal service steamer and two hydrographic survey ships and quietly acquired seven wooden trawlers from their American civilian owners, which were converted to minesweep-ers to keep the harbour approaches clear. The RCN had ordered twelve minesweeping

*Good examples of the RCN's First World War fleet of patrol craft, alongside at Halifax, 1918.
(L–R) Wooden drifters 16 and 22, Battle class trawler HMCS Givenchy, and patrol vessel HMCS Cartier.*

anti-submarine steel trawlers in the spring of 1917, six to be built in Montreal and six in Toronto, hoping they would be ready by the summer. The modest, forty-metre, 350-ton Battle-class vessels were named in honour of the battles and towns where soldiers of the Canadian Expeditionary Force lived, fought, and died on the Western Front. Each trawler had a crew of eighteen and mounted one 12-pounder gun.

The U-boat threat caused concern about Halifax's seaward defences and, at the insistence of the new British commander-in-chief at Halifax, Vice Admiral Sir Montague Browning, a new submarine net was installed in July. In the end, the adoption of the convoy system was a key element in the Allied victory over Germany, and Halifax was a major player in the convoys. Contrary to what had happened previously—when merely the threat of a U-boat nearby could close Halifax for hours or even days—ships now sailed on time by the most direct route and were protected during the entire crossing, usually by a navy cruiser or an armed merchant-cruiser, against German surface raiders. Anti-submarine vessels concentrated in coastal waters, where U-boats hunted their prey.

The responsibility for providing convoy protection as convoys formed and sailed from North American ports fell to RCN local escort forces, which remained woefully under-manned, underequipped, and undertrained for the task. And there was always the all-too-valid Canadian concern that the RN would try to step in to control the RCN's assets, limited as they were. It was not long in coming. Once local convoy protection became a major concern in Canadian territorial waters, the Admiralty characteristically tried to assume direct control, while ignoring Canadian autonomy. Fortunately, the RCN managed to win its case and retain control.

Although several ships had been sunk in Canadian waters during the war, the major-ity of them were fishing vessels. Their loss was certainly tragic—especially the deaths of the fishermen aboard them—but it did not hinder the war effort. Convoys were the only answer to the U-boat plague at the time and, in the end, the tiny tin-pots of the Halifax patrols made the convoys possible.

*The south gate of Halifax's HMC Dockyard, July 23, 1926. The government allowed naval facilities to run down after the First World War.*

CHAPTER 3

# AN END, AN INTERLUDE, AND A BEGINNING

## THE END OF THE FIRST WORLD WAR

A S THE WAR BEGAN to wind down, there was evidence of restlessness among naval and military personnel in Halifax. Incidents of brawling increased between residents and servicemen as well as theft by service personnel. In May 1918, an ugly episode occurred that quickly grew from a minor incident to a major one, a foreshadowing of events at the end of the Second World War on a much smaller scale. It began when a sailor was caught shoplifting by an employee of a Barrington Street store and was arrested by a beat cop. The seaman called out to his buddies, who unhesitatingly attacked the police officer. In response, the officer summoned help by blowing his whistle. As more police, sailors, and soldiers piled on, a mini-riot ensued within twenty minutes.

The mob of sailors and soldiers began beating every police officer in sight, and then chased the rest back to the police station in the basement of City Hall. Others—merchant seamen, longshoremen, prostitutes, local ne'er-do-wells—quickly joined the fray. At the time, a new marketplace was under construction on the upper side of nearby Market Street, which provided a ready supply of bricks to throw through the windows of City Hall.

Police tried to sally forth several times, but were beaten back each time by a heavy bombardment of bricks. Meanwhile, some of the mob had broken into City Hall, where they destroyed everything they could before attempting to start a fire on top of the police station, using municipal documents that they had heaped on the floor. The rioters did not succeed in this endeavour and returned to smashing windows. They fled only when a body of armed sailors and Royal Marines from an RN cruiser anchored in the harbour appeared on the scene.

By the end of the war, the RCN consisted of more than a hundred warships—although most of them were quite small—and had ninety-six hundred officers and men serving in it. In addition, it had formed a short-lived Naval Air Service—the first Canadian air force. But in the minds of most Canadians, the RCN had done little towards winning the war. It was an opinion shared by others. In 1930, the prestigious *Cambridge History of the British Empire* noted with disdain that "Canada's…naval contribution to the World War was so small…that no Canadian naval history need be recorded here."

Instead, it was the soldiers of the Canadian Corps, the victors at Vimy Ridge and the Empire's shock troops of the closing battles of the war, known as Canada's Hundred Days, who received the accolades of politicians and the public, both at home and abroad. It remained to be seen if the government had learned any lessons about sea power during the war, especially the need for a core of professional sailors in peacetime, as well as the necessity for a solid industrial base to build warships. Canadians would find the answer soon enough—and it was certainly not what the navy wanted.

After four long, hard years of war, the last thing the Canadian government and the Canadian people wanted to think about was the future of the armed forces and preparations for another war. Although the British continued to push for the idea of a single imperial navy made up of contributions from the Empire, Prime Minister Borden refused outright to consider such a proposal. He had been blindsided once too often by the self-interest of the British during the war and vowed it would not happen again. As far as the navy was concerned, Canada would go it alone.

There was a long way to go. After the war, the RCN was reduced to five hundred officers and men. All that remained at Halifax was the hulk of *Niobe*, still being used as a depot ship and bearing the scars of the 1917 explosion. She shared this latter quality with much of the dockyard, which was also in bad shape after four years of continuous overuse. The one bright spark for the navy—the establishment of the Canadian Naval Air Service—had been extinguished after just three short months of existence.

# NAVAL AVIATION TAKES FLIGHT—BRIEFLY

DURING THE RECENT WAR, another new form of warfare had made its debut against the submarine—the airplane—although generally the idea was slow to catch on. It was not until 1916 that its value against U-boats began to be realized as the British and French intensified their maritime reconnaissance patrols against Germany's underwater fleet. When the German U-boat threat was about to become a reality in North American waters in early 1918, Canada had no air force and Britain had no warplanes to spare against the underwater menace. Then the United States offered its assistance.

To sort out the issue of maritime air patrols over Canadian coastal waters, a meeting was held in Washington, D.C., on April 20, 1918, attended by representatives of the USN, RCN, and RN. Their comprehensive plan resulted in the establishment of a seaplane base at Bakers Point in Eastern Passage in August of that year. The conference also proposed the establishment of a Canadian Naval Air Service, which the Canadian cabinet subsequently approved. On September 5, the Royal Canadian Naval Air Service (RCNAS) came into existence. Pay included a risk allowance of a dollar a day.

In the meantime, Acting Lieutenant Commander Richard Evelyn Byrd, Jr.—later to achieve worldwide fame as a polar aviator and explorer—had been appointed officer-in-charge, United States Naval Air Force in Canada. He received orders to report for duty to Halifax, as commanding officer of the USN air station there, which did not yet exist—he would have to establish it. Using Curtiss HS-2L flying boats, supported by six submarine

*Launching a Curtiss HS-2L flying boat at Bakers Point, 1918.*

*A pilot sits in the cockpit of his Curtiss HS-2L flying boat at Bakers Point, 1918.*

chasers, two torpedo boats, and a submarine, the Americans were to patrol off the harbour approaches for enemy submarines and provide convoy escorts. In early August, Byrd arrived in Halifax along with the first men of his detachment and several train carloads of equipment. The airbase at Bakers Point had begun.

On August 19, 1918, the hoisting of the Stars and Stripes signalled the commissioning of Byrd's command. Four Curtiss flying boats were soon assembled, and on August 25, two of them made their initial flights over the startled citizens of Halifax. A letter sent the next day from the garrison's senior military staff officer to the naval authorities indicates just how surprised they were and requested information in advance of future flights "as the fortress is equipped with anti-aircraft defences."

*The seaplane base at Bakers Point, c.1920.*

Byrd worked out a patrol plan with Canadian and British naval authorities on August 26. Europe-bound fast convoys would be met off the harbour mouth and escorted 105 kilometres out to sea, while Halifax-bound ones would be met 130 kilometres out and escorted into the harbour. Slower convoys, those making less than eight knots, would have air cover for 80 kilometres outbound and 95 kilometres inbound.

Patrols from Bakers Point started immediately and built up an impressive log of flying hours in convoy protection, spotting for harbour defence guns, and coastal surveillance for U-boats. With four planes available initially, Byrd developed a policy that two were to be used for convoy escorts, one for emergency anti-submarine operations, and one in reserve. Each plane could remain airborne for four hours, cruising at sixty knots.

During the period from May to October 1918, five German subs operated in the area between Newfoundland and Cape Hatteras, three of them simultaneously from August to October. Between them, they managed to sink 110,000 tons of Allied shipping before they were recalled. In spite of sighting reports, none were ever seen by any of Byrd's aircraft. By the end of the war, the station was operating its full establishment of six flying boats, as well as two balloons. These balloons were operated from the Canadian hydrographic survey ship *Acadia*, which had been fitted with special winches and had earlier served as an RCN patrol and escort vessel.

With the declaration of the armistice on November 11, Byrd was ordered to turn the two stations over to the Canadians and return to Washington. When Byrd and his men departed over the next few months, they left aircraft, equipment, and buildings to be taken over by the RCNAS, a force only authorized on September 5. Unfortunately, this group was very short-lived. With the end of the war and the process of demobilization, the plans for the development of the RCNAS were halted after only three months of existence. In a memorandum, the Minister of the Naval Service noted that the RCNAS had not been abolished, but only discontinued until such time as the government decided on a policy for a permanent air service. This came in 1924 with the creation of the RCAF. Naval aviation was to remain on the back burner for several more years.

The base at Bakers Point officially closed on January 7, 1919. Negotiations between the two countries led the American government to donate twelve flying boats, twenty-six liberty aircraft engines, and four kite balloons to Canada, worth about $600,000. In turn, Canada purchased all United States ground equipment, including buildings and land, for $811,168.

Construction activity continued at Bakers Point into February 1919 to finish buildings not yet completed: a one-hundred-man barracks, a combined mess and recreation hall for three hundred personnel, and a large stores building. Then the station was virtually put into mothballs under a schedule of routine care and maintenance by civilian workers. The war was over; people were tired of military activity and welcomed peace. Few, especially those in government, wanted to think about future conflicts or the equipment to fight them.

In May 1919, the Laurentide Company, a Quebec pulp and paper manufacturer, borrowed two of the flying boats to survey the St. Maurice River valley. Stuart Graham, a former RN pilot, flew the machines from Eastern Passage to their operating base at Lac-à-la-Tortue, where they engaged in aerial photography and forest fire patrols. The local First Nations residents of the Senneterre Reserve called them *kitchi chghee* or "big duck." The beginnings of naval aviation in Canada had come to an abrupt and anticlimactic end.

## THE RUMP OF A NAVY

ADMIRAL LORD JELLICOE VISITED Canada in 1919, part of his round-the-Empire trip to advise the dominions and the colonies on their navies. For Canada, the options he presented ranged from four million dollars (four destroyers, eight submarines, eight anti-submarine patrol boats, four minesweepers) to twenty million dollars (two battle cruisers, two aircraft carriers, seven cruisers, thirteen destroyers, sixteen submarines, local defence vessels, auxiliaries). But cabinet was looking for an even better bargain, and opted for surplus RN ships that were on offer at no cost.

To replace *Niobe*, which was sold for scrap in 1920, the RCN received the Arethusa class light cruiser *Aurora* later the same year, with an RN captain remaining in command. At the same time, the navy also obtained the 1916-vintage sister destroyers *Patriot* and

HMCS Patriot *at sea, 1924. The destroyer was part of the second batch of ships the Royal Canadian Navy received from the Royal Navy in 1920, replacing the obsolete* Niobe *and* Rainbow.

*Patrician*, commanded by RCN lieutenants who had served with the RN since their time as midshipmen. Two H-class submarines, *CH-14* and *CH-15*, which the RN had presented to the RCN in February 1919, completed the navy. After the three modern surface ships arrived in Halifax on December 21, 1920, they immediately sailed on a training cruise to the West Coast via the Caribbean and returned on July 30, 1921.

In 1922, the new Liberal government of Mackenzie King, who had a deep dislike for things military, slashed the forces' budget. The RCN's share was a reduction of $1 million, from $2.5 million to $1.5 million. The new head of the navy, Commodore Walter Hose, faced the stark reality of simply keeping his force alive. What could he do?

## THE NAVAL RESERVE

HOSE'S SOLUTION WAS TO take a page from the army's book, by bringing the navy to the people. Militia units had existed for years in cities, towns, and villages across the country, with the end result that Canadians were familiar with—and supported—their soldiers. He decided to establish the Royal Canadian Naval Volunteer Reserve (RCNVR). Such an organization would not only teach Canadians what a navy was all about, it would also provide a pool of trained manpower in case of war.

To find the money to fund his scheme, Hose paid off *Aurora* and the two submarines, which were sold for scrap in 1927. He also closed the Youth Training Establishment for young sailors in Halifax, as well as the Naval College, which had been operating on the West Coast since the 1917 explosion damaged the former hospital housing it in Halifax. That left the two destroyers as the only seagoing ships in the RCN, although two trawlers were also stationed on each coast between 1922 and 1931. The destroyer *Patriot* remained at Halifax, while *Patrician* sailed to Esquimalt. Both vessels were used almost exclusively to train the new reserve force, at least in the years when there was enough money for them to put to sea. One year, sailors were sent to Bermuda to train with the RN's British

*Commodore Walter Hose succeeded Kingsmill as the director of the Naval Service in 1921.*

North America and West Indies Squadron on a Canadian National Steamships vessel because there was no money for fuel.

Operating on a shoestring, the new reserve units were established as fifteen half companies of fifteen men each and grew steadily, helped considerably by donations in cash and kind by naval-minded Canadians from coast to coast. By late 1939, twenty-one Naval Reserve Divisions consisting of two thousand officers and men were in existence, including one in Halifax.

## THE HALIFAX HALF COMPANY

TODAY'S NAVAL RESERVE DIVISION IN HALIFAX, HMCS *Scotian*, had its beginnings in the Halifax Half Company, established in 1925 under the command of Lieutenant J. P. Connolly. The unit was initially located in the dockyard and had a complement of two officers and fifty men. Sailors received twenty-five cents each time they appeared for drill parade and were provided with a bizarre mixture of uniform items, including wartime flat caps. Their naval collars had wavy tapes stitched around the edge, to distinguish them from the permanent force sailors, who had straight tapes. Similarly, the rank on officers' sleeves was wavy gold rings, patterned after the Royal Navy Volunteer Reserve. These different stripes and rings resulted in the reserves being known as the "Wavy Navy."

*The Halifax Half Company, formed in 1925, was the RCN's first reserve unit in Halifax. It later became HMCS* Scotian *and was quartered on Gottingen Street for a time.*

A similar rank insignia distinction was extended to the Royal Canadian Naval Reserve (RCNR), which consisted of trained merchant marine officers and men who had agreed to serve in the navy in an emergency. Their officer ranks were indicated by rings of narrow interwoven gold lace. Only regular force officers were entitled to wear the solid straight rings with their executive curl. The differences in rank insignia were a straight copy from the British system and probably had no place in the more relaxed Canadian way of doing things, where such divisive distinctions seemed to smack of a class consciousness relatively unknown in this country.

It is hardly surprising that the RN should be copied, given that most Canadian officers had served in RN ships and aspired to the British model, including the adoption of a British accent. The Canadians even modified a humorous British adage and made it their own: "The RCN are gentlemen trying to be seamen, the RCNR are seamen trying to be gentlemen; the RCNVR are neither trying to be both." Yet, when war came, the "Wavy Navy" was clearly in the majority.

While RCNVR ratings had their uniforms supplied, the officers had to buy their own—and received no pay to offset the cost. It was an expensive proposition, as an officer had to acquire a regular blue uniform, greatcoat, raincoat, ceremonial frock coat, sword, mess jacket, and several sets of high-collared summer whites. Whenever possible, new reserve officers purchased them second-hand to save money.

After several changes of location within the dockyard, the Halifax Half Company moved to a new Navy League building on Barrington Street in 1927, where it spent a dozen years before moving back to the dockyard just before the outbreak of the Second World War. When the war started in September 1939, the entire half company volunteered for active service and its operations were suspended temporarily.

## NEW SHIPS

IN 1928, THE RCN ACQUIRED two more hand-me-down former RN destroyers to replace the worn-out *Patriot* and *Patrician*, which were sold for scrap the next year. Commissioned in 1919, HMCS *Champlain* (ex-*Torbay*) steamed into Halifax Harbour in the company of HMCS *Vancouver* (ex-*Toreador*), which promptly sailed for the West Coast. Like *Patriot* and *Patrician*, they provided training for reservists. *Champlain* and *Vancouver* were paid off in 1936 and sold for scrap the next year. Meanwhile, Hose somehow managed to obtain approval for two new ships to be built according to RCN specifications, a first. Thanks to Hose's foresight and persistence, the RCN would enter the Second World War in far better condition than if its fortunes had been left to penny-pinching politicians alone. Hose lived to be ninety and died in his sleep in 1965. By then, he had spent more time on pension than he had in the navy, a source of great satisfaction to him.

*The ship's company of* HMCS Champlain *poses at Halifax with their ship as a backdrop, early 1930s.*

As no Canadian shipyard was capable of constructing the new ships Hose wanted, the order went to a British firm in 1929. Fortunately, the contract was signed before the stock market crash, which ushered in the Great Depression. The design requirements for these new destroyers—HMC Ships *Saguenay* and *Skeena*—which were based on the RN's A class, recognized the nature of the ice-infested waters of the North Atlantic, where these ships were most likely to spend much of their time. Specifications included hull strengthening, extra stability to deal with icing, and steam heat. Some thought was also given to the conditions in which the ratings lived, virtually unchanged since the days of sail. Sailors lived in open messdecks where they slung their hammocks, stowed their gear, ate their meals, and spent their off-watch time. Showers, improved ventilation, and additional refrigeration improved living conditions for all, much better than on RN ships. When the two warships were commissioned in 1931, they were promptly dubbed the "Rolls-Royce" destroyers.

*Saguenay* and *Skeena* arrived at Halifax on July 3, 1931, and *Skeena* departed for her West Coast base at Esquimalt in August. She returned to Halifax in 1937 and remained there until after the war started, when both ships were transferred to escort duties elsewhere. During the war, they both met with unfortunate fates. On December 1, 1940, *Saguenay* was torpedoed by the Italian submarine *Argo* 480 kilometres west of Ireland while escorting a convoy. Somehow, with her bows wrecked and twenty-one dead, she managed to make Barrow-in-Furness, England, for repairs, largely under her own power.

*The River class destroyers* Skeena, Saguenay, *and* St. Laurent *in Hamilton Harbour, Bermuda, April 1937.*

After lengthy repairs, *Saguenay* was reassigned to the Newfoundland Escort Force and on November 15, 1942, was accidentally rammed by the Panamanian freighter *Azra* south of Cape Race, Newfoundland. *Saguenay's* depth charges exploded, blowing off her stern. Repairs were made at Saint John, New Brunswick, which included sealing off her stern. *Saguenay* was then taken to HMCS *Cornwallis*, the huge new naval training base in the Annapolis Valley, where she served as a training ship from October 1943 until the end of the war.

*Skeena's* eventual fate was not much better than *Saguenay's*, although she managed to remain in action longer. In June 1940, she was involved in the evacuation of Allied forces from France, followed by escort duties in British waters and the mid-Atlantic. On July 31, 1942, while escorting convoy ON-115, she shared in the sinking of *u-588* with the corvette HMCS *Wetaskiwin*. She was later assigned to invasion of France duties and took part in D-Day on June 6, 1944. Off Iceland on October 25 that year, *Skeena* dragged her anchors in a storm and was wrecked on Videy Island, near Reykjavik.

*HMCS* Fraser *was acquired in 1937 and sank after a collision with another ship in 1940.*

In 1937, the c class destroyers HMC Ships *Fraser* (ex-*Crescent*) and *St. Laurent* (ex-*Cygnet*) were purchased from the RN as replacements for *Champlain* and *Vancouver*, to be joined the next year by HMC Ships *Restigouche* (ex-*Comet*) and *Ottawa* (ex-*Crusader*). Like many of the RCN's ships, their crews gave them colourful nicknames, usually based on some form of the ships' original names. *St. Laurent* was "Sally" and *Restigouche* was "Rustyguts." In RCN service, they soon became known as River class destroyers.

All four ships were based at Halifax at various times during the Second World War, but also ranged much further afield. Only *St. Laurent* survived the war unscathed. After the evacuation of France in June 1940, *Fraser* was en route to Bordeaux when she collided with the cruiser HMS *Calcutta* in the Gironde River estuary on June 25, losing forty-seven of her crew. Coincidentally, *Restigouche* was involved in the rescue of survivors from *Fraser* before being assigned to mid-ocean escort duties. On December 13, 1941, she suffered storm damage that required extensive repairs before she returned to the fray. *Ottawa* was torpedoed and sunk by *u-91* in the North Atlantic while escorting convoy ON-127. She lost 114 of her complement.

*HMCS* Gaspé, *one of four Fundy class minesweepers commissioned in 1938. She served with the Halifax Local Defence Force throughout the war.*

In 1938, four modern Fundy class minesweepers—*Fundy*, *Gaspé*, *Comox*, and *Nootka* (renamed *Nanoose* in 1943)—were commissioned. They had been built in various Canadian yards and initially two served on each coast. In March 1940, the two West Coast ships were transferred to Halifax to join the others on minesweeping duties with the Halifax Local Defence Force, which all four spent the rest of the war doing.

When the war began, the RCN consisted of these six destroyers and four minesweepers, along with the sail training schooner *Venture*, the training ship *Skidegate*, and the Battle class trawler *Armentières*, a relic of the First World War. One of the navy's first acts once the war broke out was to recommission seven of these trawlers, six of them as gate vessels in Nova Scotia. *Venture*, built in Meteghan on Nova Scotia's French Shore, was the only sailing vessel in the RCN's fleet at the time and was similar to *Bluenose* but had three masts instead of two. She was paid off and used until November 1941 as an accommodation vessel for ratings on the staff of the commander of the RN's 3rd Battleship Squadron at Halifax. She then became the Bedford Basin guard ship, stationed at Tufts Cove. *Skidegate*, too small for most practical purposes, was paid off in early 1942. Once the war started, the first "new" ship acquired was HMCS *Assiniboine* (ex-*Kempenfelt*), the C class flotilla leader, which was transferred from the RN in October 1939 and quickly acquired

*Two dramatic photographs of* HMCS Assiniboine *ramming* U-210 *on August 6, 1942:*

TOP *The actual moment of ramming;* U-210's *coning tower is visible on the left.*

RIGHT *A sailor hangs on as water rushes over* Assiniboine's *decks from the ramming.*

the nickname "Bones." While escorting convoy sc-94 in August 1942, she rammed and sank *u-210*, requiring repairs at Halifax.

During the war, the navy grew to more than four hundred warships, not counting smaller auxiliaries, a number far too large to tell the many stories associated with their wartime service. The vast majority of these ships were engaged in the Battle of the Atlantic, which was fought around a series of convoys sailing between North America and Britain. Halifax, and the Royal Canadian Navy, played a pivotal role in this crucial battle.

*A convoy forms up off the Dartmouth shore, next to the Acadia Sugar Refinery. The strategically important oil refinery at Imperoyal can be seen on the point of land above the convoy.*

## CHAPTER 4

# THE COURAGE OF THE CONVOYS

### THE BATTLE OF THE ATLANTIC

IN 1939, CANADA WAS AT WAR against Germany for the second time in a generation. Halifax quickly became the closest to what could be described as front lines in
the entire country. The city and its vast harbour became an essential cog in the war
machine. It was the RCN's main port and a major station for the RN. Hundreds of troop
and supply convoys formed up in the protected waters of Bedford Basin before sailing
across the North Atlantic to England, carrying much-needed men and matériel. As it had
been during the First World War, a submarine net stretched across the mouth of the harbour to keep out German U-boats, while the outer harbour islands and the forelands on
each side of the harbour entrance were studded with defences.

*A convoy forms up in Bedford Basin, as viewed from Africville, April 1941.*

The Battle of the Atlantic was arguably the most decisive campaign of the Second World War and lasted for the entire duration of the war in Europe, from September 1939 to May 1945. By mid-1942, Canada provided about half of the convoy escorts in the North Atlantic and the lion's share thereafter, plus virtually all land-based aircraft from Newfoundland and the Maritimes.

Initially, Germany used a combination of U-boats, mines, surface raiders, and airplanes to sink ships, but Allied reaction soon left U-boats as the major German weapon. The Allies responded through an ever-increasing reliance on the proven convoy system, whose protection by escorting and patrolling warships and aircraft improved as the war went on. Eventually, Allied tactical and technical improvements, such as better detection and destruction of U-boats, breaking the German "Enigma" code, and the introduction of very long-range patrol aircraft, coupled with the rising production of replacement and new merchant shipping, won the battle. In all, the Germans sank about thirty-five hundred Allied merchant ships totalling over 15,000,000 tons, the vast majority due to U-boats. But by 1945, RCN warships—many of them based in Halifax—had escorted 25,343 merchant ships carrying more than 180,000,000 tons of cargo to Britain.

Although initial U-boat attacks were against shipping as it approached the British Isles, the area U-boats covered expanded steadily westwards. Only Hitler's reluctance to inadvertently sink American ships and bring the United States into the war prevented his submarines from mining the Halifax approaches. Initially, U-boat "wolf-pack" tactics caused losses of Allied merchant shipping to exceed new construction; for every three ships sunk, only one was replaced. In June 1941, 590,000 tons of shipping were sunk, with eleven of

*The war according to the* Star Weekly: *The fanciful cover of this popular Saturday newspaper of April 3, 1943, shows an imaginary scene of Allied battleships sinking a German destroyer. By this time, German surface raiders had already been driven from the North Atlantic.*

these ships lost within thirteen hundred kilometres of Halifax. And yet for every enemy submarine sunk, three more slid down the slipways, soon to be increased to eight. In another year, the war would come closer to Canada than ever before.

Operation *Paukenschlag* ("Drumbeat") was Hitler's strategic submarine offensive against North America. German U-boats operated off the eastern seaboard of Canada and the United States in great numbers, accounting for the destruction of much coastal shipping. Unfortunately, there was little the planners could do. The navy's resources were already stretched to the limit with local and mid-ocean escorts, and new commitments along the American coast and in the Caribbean would soon draw off additional ships. None could be spared from areas where U-boat attacks were actually taking place to go to an area where they "might" occur.

## THE CORVETTE NAVY

THE MOST UBIQUITOUS TYPE of warship in the RCN during the Second World War was the corvette, a tiny vessel that made a contribution out of proportion to its size in winning the war. The corvette story begins at Smith's Dock Company, a shipbuilder known for its whaling vessels, in South Bank, Yorkshire, England, in the mid-1930s. One of the firm's designers created a small coastal craft named Patrol Vessel, Whaler Type. In keeping with the company's whaling heritage, the vessel was seaworthy, manoeuvrable, inexpensive, and comparatively simple to construct, although they were said to "roll on heavy dew."

When the Second World War began, hundreds of escort ships were needed to protect the vulnerable North Atlantic convoy lifeline linking North America to Europe. The British Admiralty suggested that Canada construct a fleet of Patrol Vessels, Whaler Type, in keeping with the country's shipbuilding capabilities. The construction programme began in early 1940, and by the time the war ended, the RCN manned 123 corvettes, the new name by which the small vessels were known. The RN designated the corvettes as

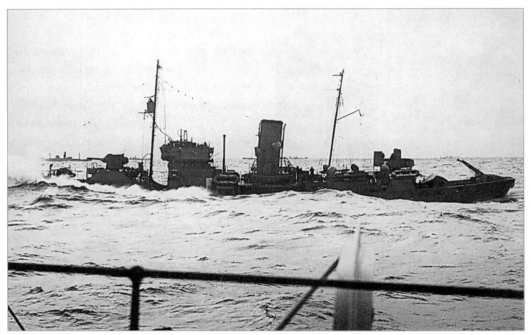

*The corvette* HMCS Battleford *on convoy escort in the North Atlantic, November 1941. She was one of 123 corvettes in the Royal Canadian Navy, 107 of which were built in Canada.*

Flower class, although all but a handful in RCN service were named after Canadian cities and towns.

The first corvettes were sixty-two metres long with a beam of ten metres and a displacement of 950 tons. A reciprocating steam engine propelled them along at a maximum speed of sixteen knots—about the same as the speed of the U-boats they hunted. Their armament consisted of a 4-inch gun, a light anti-aircraft gun, and depth charges. Initially corvettes had a crew of fifty-two, but this grew as the complexity of weapons and sensors increased during the war. Ten of these gallant little ships were lost due to enemy action during the war.

In *Through the Gates* by McNabs Island wartime resident Marguerite Harding, Harold Rafuse described corvettes with less than pleasant memories: "They were terrible, almost unbearable in rough weather," he recalled, and so small that they were not long enough to span the distance between waves. During high seas, as the bow of the ship went down the wave, the stern was at the top of the wave. As the bow climbed the next wave, the stern went down. "We had to hang on to anything available as she slammed into the rough seas, rose and fell twenty to thirty feet [seven to nine metres], and more than that in rough seas. Added to that she yawed and rolled." Corvettes were "great for

*"Ash cans away!" A corvette's main weapon against U-boats was depth charges—often with spectacular results.*

*One of the hazards of the North Atlantic was ice formed by freezing spray, which had to be kept clear of vital equipment with axes and steam hoses. If allowed to build up, ice could make a ship top-heavy and capsize her.*

getting seasick," he added, and the sailors "got used to it after awhile; [although] they were not intended for comfortable living."

Another of Harding's interviewed corvette veterans, Bernie Churchill, remembered that "during high wind, spray washed up over the deck and removed everything that wasn't fastened down." During winter, it was far worse as "the spray froze and coated everything with ice. If someone left a hatch open, as the wave broke over the ship, water poured down the hatch." He summarized his experience on corvettes as "Wet! Cold! Uncomfortable!"

## THE NAVAL CONTROL SERVICE

THE NAVAL CONTROL SERVICE (NCS) was a small group of officers and men in Halifax under Commander Dick Oland who were responsible for confirming that all merchant ships were "in all respects ready" to go to sea. They inspected ships for any explosives that enemy saboteurs might have planted aboard them—which German agents had done during the First World War—and ensured that the ships had suitable working and living conditions for their crews.

On the outbreak of the war, the NCS automatically took charge of directing merchant vessels to ports where their cargoes were most needed and setting up the convoys in which they sailed. As Halifax was the major convoy assembly port in North America, the job of inspecting every ship was huge. Tom Watt, a First World War able seaman who stayed on in the naval reserve after the war, had been promoted to lieutenant and attached to the NCS for this job. To carry it out, he had six naval reservists.

As Bill McNeil recorded in *Voices of a War Remembered: An Oral History of Canadians in World War II*, Watt was not pleased. "Since this wasn't the 'action at sea' job I had been hoping for, I was understandably disappointed," he noted. He tried to tell Oland that he knew nothing of merchant ships or anti-sabotage work, but to no avail. Oland simply pointed out that none of his men were anti-sabotage specialists either, adding optimistically that they "could all learn together." In response, Watt "set out along with my men to do the job as best we could."

They quickly found out the total impossibility of finding explosives on the ten or more fully laden ships they had to search every day, vessels that were usually berthed in widely separated locations. There was only enough time to check cargo and crew lists and conduct the occasional spot check on a hold. Fortunately, the Germans seemed to have decided against this form of sabotage and Watt and his sailors "found no explosives and apparently there were none."

But they did find something else as potentially damaging: "the truly explosive thing aboard all of these ships getting ready for convoy was the seaman's morale." During his first few weeks on the job, Watt noticed that several ships were not ready to leave with

*Officers of the RCN's Naval Control Service returning to their examination vessel after inspecting a merchant ship, Halifax, May 1942.*

*An unidentified rating of the Naval Control Service inspects the cargo of a merchant ship, Halifax, 1940.*

the scheduled convoy. "Crew trouble" was usually stated as the reason, which included a wide range of complaints such as wages, food, or accommodation. For others, "they would simply decide that they didn't want any more of the horror of life out there in the submarine zone."

Watt reported his experiences to Oland, who sent it up the chain to Ottawa. For once, the official response was swift. The number of officers and ratings in the NCS boarding parties was increased and they were ordered to provide detailed reports on crew morale and conditions aboard the ships. Legislation was enacted to deal with troublemakers, while volunteer organizations swung into action to improve the welfare of merchant seamen.

The results were immediate. Reports of crew trouble lessened dramatically and Canada's nine other ports copied the organization of the Halifax NCS. Even the RN, which generally assumed that no one could teach it anything—especially "colonials"—expressed an interest in what the RCN was doing, leading to a regular exchange of information. As the war progressed and more and more ships got through to Britain, Watt believed that the Halifax NCS "played a large part" in it.

# CONVOY ORGANIZATION

BEFORE EVERY CONVOY SAILED from Halifax, the merchant vessels' captains attended a conference, usually in Admiralty House, held by the NCS. There, they were given a copy of Convoy Sailing Orders, with details of their timings, speed, routes, station keeping, escort forces, recognition signals, weather patterns, enemy situation, and other important information. Plans had been made to establish the NCS before the war started, so once hostilities broke out it was an easy matter for the organization to get up and running quickly. HX-1, the first transatlantic slow convoy, left Halifax under escort of *St. Laurent* and *Saguenay* on September 16, while the first fast one left the next day, escorted by *Fraser*. They arrived in Britain safely, the first of many that kept open the essential lifeline to the beleaguered island nation, often against great odds and under appalling conditions.

At the start of the war, each convoy was commanded by a convoy commodore, usually a retired British admiral or commodore who had volunteered for the job. Victor Oland, a nephew of Dick Oland who headed the NCS, said that "some of them, well into their seventies, had to be helped up the side of the rusty old freighters from which they assumed

*Commander Dick Oland (tall officer, centre) briefs merchant captains and naval officers as they study their orders at a convoy conference at Admiralty House, Halifax, March 1941. Seated to Oland's left is the convoy commodore (elderly officer with broad stripe), while to his right is the RN captain of the heavy ship escort (officer with four stripes). Most merchant masters wore civilian clothes.*

*Convoy escort officers attend a tactical meeting at Halifax early in the war, conducted by Captain Wallace Creery (centre), captain-in-charge Halifax and King's Harbour Master.*

command of the convoy," he recalled in Graham Metson's *An East Coast Port: Halifax at War 1939–1945*. Oland called them "one of the finest and bravest groups of men" that he had ever known.

Line astern, the merchantmen making up a convoy would steam out of Bedford Basin, through the narrows, the inner harbour, and the outer harbour. RCAF flying boats and RCN minesweepers would already be ahead of them, searching for any signs of enemy submarines or sweeping the channel. Once clear of the submarine net, the convoy would form up into the positions it was supposed to hold until it was well inside British home waters—weather and enemy permitting. Ships carrying cargoes like lumber or wheat travelled on the outside of the convoy, while tankers and those carrying ammunition travelled in the middle.

Escort forces varied depending on availability: RCN corvettes and destroyers, an RN cruiser or battleship, a passenger liner converted into an armed merchant cruiser. Once at sea, escorts continuously patrolled ahead, astern, and along the flanks of the convoy as it zigzagged on short, middle, and long course changes during daylight, then settled into a standard nighttime course of straight ahead as no lights were shown. Inevitably, collisions occurred, especially during fog and storms.

*The armed merchant cruiser* Jervis Bay *steams towards the German pocket battleship* Admiral Scheer, *guns blazing, as the convoy scatters behind her, November 5, 1940.*

## THE SACRIFICE OF *JERVIS BAY*

ON THE FINE, CLEAR AFTERNOON of November 5, 1940, convoy HX-84 was in mid-Atlantic, four hundred kilometres south of Greenland and eight days out of Halifax, steaming towards Britain with vital war supplies of gasoline and food. Its thirty-seven ships were spread out in nine columns under the sole escort of HMS *Jervis Bay*, an eighteen-year-old, 14,000-ton Australian passenger liner converted to an armed merchant cruiser, fitted out with seven 6-inch guns. *Jervis Bay* had spent the summer in dry dock in Saint John, New Brunswick, preparing for her new role.

Late that afternoon as he scanned the seas, Midshipman Ronnie Butler reported to his captain, "Ship to port, sir, on the horizon." Captain Edward Stephen Fogarty Fegen, the forty-nine-year-old RN officer and First World War veteran commanding *Jervis Bay*, got the vessel in his glasses and immediately gave the order "Sound 'Action Stations.' Enemy raider. Tell convoy to scatter and make smoke."

The stranger was *Admiral Scheer*, a 10,000-ton German commerce-raiding pocket battleship, armed with six 11-inch guns and eight 5.9-inch guns. At about 5:10 PM, at a range of more than fifteen kilometres, *Scheer* opened fire, her first rounds landing in the middle of the convoy lanes. Fegen's seven guns had a maximum range of nine kilometres. "You wouldn't believe it," Robert Squires, a Canadian crew member recalled, "but our 6-inch guns were made in 1899 and 1900 for the Boer War." Undeterred, Fegen immediately broke out of the convoy, "action stations" clanging, and headed straight for *Scheer* at full speed, firing as he went. He knew full well there could be but one end to this uneven battle, yet his duty was to protect the convoy.

*Scheer*'s third salvo hit *Jervis Bay*'s bridge, setting it on fire and shattering Fegen's right arm. The one-sided battle quickly turned into a massacre. In quick succession, *Jervis Bay*'s fire control, range finder, steering gear, and radio were knocked out. Fegen staggered to the after bridge, blood dripping from his arm, in an attempt to control his ship, but when it was blown away he was forced to return to the wrecked fore bridge.

*Jervis Bay*'s superstructure was hit repeatedly and her hull holed in several places as fires raged from stem to stern. Any guns not already destroyed continued to blaze away, but even at full elevation they fell short of the German raider, which stayed outside the range of Fegen's guns. Soon *Jervis Bay* began to list heavily and her decks were awash. As one survivor recalled, "It was an inferno—flying shell and flame all over the place."

On the main bridge, Fegen, severely wounded, gasped out "Abandon ship!" As the surviving crew scrambled into the four remaining undamaged life rafts, *Jervis Bay* settled by the stern. Even when she lay dead in the water, a burning hulk, *Scheer* continued to send broadside after broadside into her. As *Jervis Bay* slowly went down, Fegen stood on the

*Seven Canadian sailors who survived the sinking of* Jervis Bay *give a happy thumbs-up after arriving safely in Halifax, November 12, 1940.*

bridge, arms hanging limply at his side. When she slipped beneath the waves about eight o'clock, almost three hours after *Scheer*'s first salvo, her colours were still flying. But the terrible ordeal was not yet over, as *Scheer* began firing at the men on the life rafts, wounding nearly all of them.

The gallant self-sacrifice of Fegen and the majority of his crew was not in vain. The delay saved most of the convoy as its ships escaped in different directions. *Scheer* pursued and sank five of them, but thirty-one got away. Of *Jervis Bay*'s complement of 254 officers and men, a mixed bag of RN and RCN regulars and merchant navy, 65 were rescued and brought to Halifax, arriving on November 12. The Swedish freighter *Stureholm*, one of the ships in the convoy, had remained in the area looking for survivors rather than scrambling to safety and had witnessed the uneven battle.

In Halifax, Captain Sven Olander, the *Stureholm*'s skipper, said, "Never will I forget the gallantry of that British captain sailing forward to meet the enemy." When the survivors told what happened, the story of *Jervis Bay* electrified the free world. Fegen's posthumous Victoria Cross, "for valour in challenging hopeless odds and giving his life to save the many ships it was his duty to protect," was announced a few days later.

Royal Naval officers reported the bravery of the Canadian sailors aboard was "a wonderful example of the courage and spirit of the Canadian navy." The fifteen who went down with the ship are commemorated on the Sailors' Memorial in Halifax's Point Pleasant Park. Even British Prime Minister Winston Churchill paid tribute to this "forlorn and heroic action." A month later, *Stureholm* was torpedoed by *U-96* off the west coast of Scotland and lost with all hands, including Olander.

## CARIBBEAN DUTY

THE PROVISION OF SUFFICIENT OIL and other petroleum products to run the industry and machines of war was a problem throughout the conflict. A concerted effort by U-boats against Allied shipping in the Caribbean Sea and Gulf of Mexico in 1942 resulted in the sinking of 121 ships in June alone, most of them tankers. Ships, their cargoes, and—most important of all—their experienced crews, were being lost at an alarming and irreplaceable rate. The ensuing shortage of oil at Halifax and in Britain resulted in the establishment of temporary fast tanker convoys between Halifax and Trinidad, and then between Halifax and Aruba. Virtually all of the escorts for these convoys were provided by RCN ships from Halifax and involved seven corvettes that were taken off mid-ocean duties. Between May and August 1942, HMC Ships *Fredericton*, *Halifax*, *Hepatica*, *Oakville*, *Snowberry*, *Sudbury*, and *The Pas* escorted thirty-two of these tanker convoys, five of which had Key West, Florida, as their final destination.

For the corvette crews, cloudless blues skies, bright sun, and deep azure seas were a welcome change from the overcast skies, fog, and storms of the North Atlantic. Tropical dress—sunhats, white shirts, and shorts with sandals—became the order of the day as awnings were stretched over the bridge and other parts of the ships for shade. The odd run ashore found palm tree–lined white beaches, cooling tropical drinks, and beautiful girls to round out the crews' good fortune.

Sub-Lieutenant Hal Lawrence sailed in *Oakville* under Lieutenant Commander Clarence King, who had won a Distinguished Service Cross in the First World War for sinking a U-boat. Lawrence described his Caribbean adventures in his postwar reminiscences, *A Bloody War*. On August 25, *Oakville* departed Port of Spain, Trinidad, with the twenty-nine ships of fast convoy TAW-15, heading for Key West. The escort force consisted of the American destroyer USS *Lea*, *Oakville* and two other RCN corvettes (*Halifax* and *Snowberry*), a Dutch corvette, and three small USN patrol craft. On the night of August 28, having picked up additional tankers at Aruba and Curaçao, the convoy was south of Haiti, about to enter the Windward Passage, separating that country from Cuba.

Oberleutenant Otto Ites had spotted TAW-15 and was proceeding dead-slow on the convoy's port bow in *U-94*, with only his conning tower awash. The twenty-four-year-old Ites had four years in submarines under his belt and had already sunk more than 100,000 tons of shipping. Overhead, a USN Catalina patrol aircraft, unseen by Ites, spotted the sub and swooped in to drop four depth bombs and a flare. *U-94* dove as action stations

*The tiny anti-submarine cabin of a corvette was a crowded place to work, in this case HMCS* Cobourg, *Halifax, July 13, 1944.*

sounded on *Oakville*, running towards the flare at full speed. When she reached the spot where the aircraft's depth bombs exploded, King ordered a five-charge pattern of depth charges fired.

Lawrence pressed the fire-bell and a depth charge arched outwards from either side, while three more dropped from stern racks. "With a rumble they exploded," he recalled. "Water erupted to mast-head height. *Oakville* bucked, shuddered, and resumed her eager trembling." The depth charges had found their target, and through the asdic operator's headphones came the unmistakable sound of a sub blowing her ballast tanks so she could surface. Just then, "A black snout reared out of the water. The conning tower burst through a swell and she surfaced completely. Water cascaded from her decks, white and foamy in the moonlight."

King ordered, "Stand by to ram," but the resulting attack only struck a glancing blow because of the short distance in which the corvette's captain had to manoeuvre. He came around for another run-in as *Oakville*'s 4-inch gun, 20-mm Oerlikon, and .50-calibre machine guns blasted away, registering hits on the conning tower and hull as German sailors poured out of the sub and ran for their deck guns. Ites had *U-94* underway by now and manoeuvred skilfully to avoid being rammed. *Oakville* struck the sub another

*Lieutenant Hal Lawrence (left) and Stoker Petty Officer Art Powell in Halifax, October 17, 1942, after the sinking of* U-94 *that August.*

glancing blow. As the two vessels passed alongside each other only six metres apart, some of *Oakville*'s stokers, who were on deck watching the action as they waited to reload the depth charge throwers, began pelting the submariners with well-aimed empty Coke bottles that had been stowed abaft the funnel.

King fired depth charges again, one of which exploded directly under *u-94*. The submarine reared up and then slowed down. King came around for a third ramming as the corvette's guns continued to chatter away. *Oakville* struck the sub at right angles, her bow lifted; *u-94* rolled under and popped up astern, wallowing and dead in the water. "Away boarding party," King bellowed. "Come on, Lawrence. Get cracking!"

In response, Lawrence quickly assembled the twelve men designated as the corvette's boarding party and struggled into the appropriate gear along with the rest of them, all dressed only in tropical shorts or underwear, plus the odd pair of gym shoes, because of the hot night. As the sailors mustered, King yelled out not to bother lowering the boat, as he would bring his vessel alongside the sub. In view of the captain's two misses, Lawrence regarded his statement somewhat sceptically.

But King was as good as his word, and Lawrence and Stoker Petty Officer Art Powell dropped onto the U-boat's deck some 2½ to 3 metres lower, each armed with a .45-calibre pistol. Unfortunately, as Lawrence's feet hit the deck, the impact snapped the belt of his tropical shorts and they slid down to his ankles. He stood up, kicked them off and, wearing only his lifebelt, set off to capture the crew.

After getting the German sailors under control—which included shooting two of them—Lawrence went down the hatch to try and close the scuttling valves. But it was dark below and already too late. Lawrence, Powell, and the Germans jumped into the water. As he swam away, Lawrence looked back. "We hadn't abandoned *u-94* too soon; she lifted her bow, and slid under." It was only forty-five minutes after the sub had first been sighted.

*Oakville* had suffered serious damage as well, with much of her bottom torn away and water flooding in through various breaches. The crew struggled to make temporary repairs to stop the flow. Of *u-94*'s crew of forty-five, nineteen were dead, leaving twenty-six to be landed at Guantanamo, Cuba. *Oakville*'s only casualty was Lawrence; as he wriggled down *u-94*'s hatch, he cut his elbow on a broken Coke bottle. For their heroism, King added the Distinguished Service Order to his earlier Distinguished Service Cross, Lawrence received the Distinguished Service Cross, and Powell was awarded the Distinguished Service Medal. The dramatic battle between *Oakville* and *u-94* was only one of many short, sharp actions in which sailors of the RCN excelled during the war.

*Two First World War Battle class trawlers,* HMC Ships *Festubert (pictured) and* Ypres, *served as gate vessels at the entrance to Halifax Harbour during the Second World War. Their job was to open and close the gate in the anti-submarine net to allow friendly vessels in and out of the harbour.*

CHAPTER 5

# DEATH AND DESTRUCTION ON HALIFAX'S DOORSTEP

### NIGHT OF THE *CARIBOU*

AS FAR AS MOST CANADIANS ARE CONCERNED, the Second World War was an event that took place somewhere else. No enemy troops invaded Canada and no enemy airplanes bombed our cities. But it is wrong to think Canadians were safe behind our ocean barriers from attacks by our adversaries. Those very oceans that kept the soldiers and bombs of our opponents from our shores brought another enemy to them—U-boats from the mighty German underwater fleet. Many of those struck close to home.

During the summer and early fall of 1942, the Second World War at sea had gone badly for Canada. Half a dozen German submarines operated freely in the Gulf of St. Lawrence and sank twenty ships without any losses themselves. Faced with a rising toll of lives and ships, the government closed the gulf to transatlantic shipping and limited coastal convoys to essential levels. One of the routes that remained open was the Sydney to Port aux Basques ferry run, where the ferry *Caribou* continued to ply her peacetime route. On the night of October 14, 1942, while *Caribou* was under escort of the minesweeper HMCS *Grandmère*, *U-69* attacked her in the Cabot Strait, just sixty-five kilometres from her Newfoundland destination.

Running in on the surface ahead of the ferry in good visibility, *U-69* fired a single torpedo at short range, which quickly found its mark. Of the 119 civilians and 118 military personnel aboard, only 101 were rescued. The ferry's captain and his two sons perished, as well as five mothers and ten children. Two RCN nursing sisters were aboard: Sub-Lieutenant Agnes Wilkie became the only Canadian nurse to die due to enemy action during the war. Her companion, Sub-Lieutenant Margaret Brooke, struggled for over two hours to hold on to Wilkie and the ropes of an overturned life raft. She was appointed a Member of the Order of the British Empire for her gallant efforts to save Wilkie.

## NOT-SO-SWEET REVENGE

IT IS DIFFICULT FOR US today to realize to what extent Nova Scotia, bordering as it does on some of the world's major sea lanes, was an armed camp during the Second World War. Halifax, the start point and destination for hundreds of transatlantic convoys, bristled with harbour defences against seaborne or airborne attack: booms and anti-submarine nets, minefields and underwater torpedoes, searchlights and anti-aircraft guns.

Strangely enough, the loss of the RCN's first ship off Halifax had nothing to do with enemy action, but was caused by an RN battleship. HMCS *Ypres*, one of twelve 350-ton Battle class anti-submarine trawlers built to deal with German U-boats during the First World War, had been recommissioned in 1938. Along with her sister ship, HMCS *Festubert*, she was used as a gate vessel to open and close the gate in the Halifax Harbour defences, where her station was off Maugers Beach. She was commanded by Lieutenant Antoine Cassivi.

The harbour defences consisted of two lines of heavy wire rope net hanging vertically from a series of large buoys. The nets were anchored to the bottom and stretched from McNabs Island to the western shore. In the middle was a boom gate of similar material, which could be opened and closed by the gate vessels and which acted on orders from shore authorities. The gate was wide enough for the very largest ships to pass through in single file.

On the afternoon of May 12, 1940, troop convoy TC-4A was preparing to depart for Britain. It consisted of the liners *Duchess of Bedford* and *Antonia*, escorted by HMS *Revenge*, an antiquated 33,500-ton battleship. Due to departure difficulties, an original 7:00 sailing

*A double line of submarine nets stretches from the shore below York Redoubt to Maugers Beach on McNabs Island. The two gate vessels in the centre have opened the gate in the net to let a merchant ship out of the harbour, May 1942.*

was postponed until 8:15, about fifteen minutes before sunset. Neither the officer responsible for gate operations nor the two gate vessels were advised of this change. When the battleship and her charges did not show up on time, *Ypres* and *Festubert* closed the gate on their own around 7:20. It was raining at the time and visibility was limited. During periods of darkness and poor visibility one gate vessel showed a red light to indicate the gate was closed, while a green one meant it was open. At 8:46 authorities ordered the gate opened. Although *Ypres* reported the gate fully open at 8:55, *Revenge*'s log recorded that at 8:49 the boom gate was shut and full astern was ordered; two minutes later it noted she struck the starboard gate vessel. The glancing blow rolled *Ypres* almost over on her side and water poured in through her upper deck openings.

The momentum of 33,500 tons travelling at eight knots meant the battleship could not stop in time, so when *Revenge*'s commander, Captain E. R. Archer—appropriately nicknamed "Rammer" by his crew—realized that the gate was still closed, he decided that hitting the gate vessel would cause the least damage to his ship and the shortest delay to the convoy. As *Revenge* continued to plough through, the gate became caught on her stem. *Ypres* was secured to the gate's cables, so she was pulled along, bounced off the battleship's

*The Royal Navy's First World War–vintage battleship* HMS Revenge *was a sister ship of* HMS Resolution *(pictured). During the Second World War, she was used to escort convoys across the Atlantic Ocean.*

bow, and smashed against her hull. By then *Ypres* was listing forty to fifty degrees and had been dragged about 460 metres beyond the net when *Revenge* finally stopped.

Lieutenant Cassivi gave the order to abandon ship. Fortunately, the gate vessel did not sink at once, so the crew were able to get off in good order, although in some haste. Meanwhile, *Revenge*'s crew hauled thirteen sailors from *Ypres* out of the water and *Festubert*'s skiff picked up the other five. One British sailor even jumped overboard to save a Canadian seaman.

*Ypres* went down at about 9:25, and a minute later, having ascertained there was no loss of life, *Revenge* and the liners sailed away. The next day, the gate, buoys, and net were recovered and the gate was operating a few hours later. Authorities decided not to recover *Ypres*, given her age and probable damage from the incident, and she was demolished where she lay. No signs of her remain on the bottom today.

A Board of Inquiry into the sinking backed away from assigning any blame—especially against an RN captain—and attributed the sinking to "errors of communication." The crews of the gate vessels felt differently. Any time *Revenge* subsequently entered Halifax Harbour, they made a great show of donning life jackets and manned the upper decks in an elaborate and exaggerated abandon-ship drill as the battleship passed by. The loss of the RCN's first vessel during the war clearly showed that the Germans were not the only danger sailors faced; sometimes an ally could be as much of a threat.

## ORDEAL BY FIRE

LIKE *YPRES*, THE RCN'S SECOND WARSHIP loss off Halifax was also not the result of enemy action. HMCS *Otter* was the former fifty-metre civilian yacht *Conseco*, launched in New York in 1921, bought secretly in the United States, taken into navy service in 1940,

HMCS Otter *in the process of conversion from the private yacht* Conseco. *No known photograph exists of* Otter *as a naval vessel.*

and turned into a coastal patrol vessel armed with a 3-inch gun. She served as a local escort for convoys, as well as patrolling back and forth across the entrance to Halifax Harbour, searching for floating mines and German U-boats.

At 5:00 AM on March 26, 1941, *Otter* left the dockyard and took up station sixteen hundred metres from the Sambro Light Vessel, about thirty-two kilometres off Halifax, to meet an inbound RN submarine, HMS *Talisman*. Most ports did this when friendly submarines were due, to prevent them from being mistaken for a U-boat and attacked by nervous defenders. The day was cold, wet, and windy. Around 8:45, the sound of an explosion awakened the few sleeping off-duty sailors in *Otter*, who had somehow managed to catch a few winks in the midst of a gale-force sou'easter. They quickly joined their comrades already fighting a fire that had broken out in the engine room and soon spread flames through the wooden deck above it.

The minimal firefighting equipment aboard—sand buckets and fire extinguishers—had no effect on the fire. Soon the heat and dense, choking smoke were so intense that the crew abandoned any thoughts of saving the ship; their thoughts turned to simply saving themselves. The captain gave the order to abandon ship at 8:55 and the crew quickly made for two small dinghies and Carley float life raft.

Eleven sailors scrambled into Lifeboat No. 1 as it was being lowered over the side into the wind-whipped waves. Fortunately, the 3,100-ton Polish bulk carrier *Wisla* was passing by and saw the lifeboat. Her crewmen lowered rope ladders over the side for the stricken sailors to climb aboard. Just as one of *Otter's* sailors grabbed a ladder, a huge wave crashed into the lifeboat and flipped it over, tossing its occupants into the cold water.

As the sailors strained to right their capsized lifeboat, the Polish crew desperately lowered their two lifeboats over the side. But the strong wind smashed both boats against the freighter's hull, shattering them. Stoker Jimmy Noade, twenty-four, of Halifax, was one of the sailors in the water. Suddenly, one of his struggling shipmates grabbed him, pulling them both beneath the waves. "I wanted to save him," Noade recalled later in a *Halifax Mail* article, "but it was all I could do to save myself." When the frantic sailor would not let go, Noade pushed him away and swam to the surface, gasping for breath. He never saw his fellow crewman again. A large Eagle Oil tanker also appeared on the scene and pumped oil over the side in an attempt to flatten the waves and make any rescue easier.

After an hour in the water, somehow Noade and three others—Lieutenant Alan Walker, Chief Motor Mechanic Daniel Gillis, and Tommy Ward—managed to right the capsized lifeboat and crawl into it. They sat there, in freezing water up to their waists, exhausted from their ordeal. As Noade cradled the weakened thirty-year-old lieutenant in his arms, his fellow Haligonian asked plaintively, "Is there anything in sight?" The stoker replied, "Yes, there's a freighter," referring to the Polish vessel. Then, Noade recalled, "His head fell forward and he died in my arms."

When Gillis died next, Noade said that he and Ward "played 'patty-cake' to keep up the circulation in our arms and keep warm." Although the lifeboat was again near the Polish ship's rope ladders, neither of its occupants had the strength to grab hold. Then, one the freighter's crewmen, Able Seaman M. Ptzybliski, stepped in, tied a rope around his waist, and had his shipmates lower him into the battered lifeboat.

In the tossing small boat, Ptzybliski tied his rope around Tommy Ward and signalled his fellow sailors to haul him aboard. Noade followed. The lifeless bodies of Walker and Gillis were next. On deck, the Polish crew took turns administering artificial respiration and rubbing the still bodies with alcohol, in a futile attempt to warm them. After two hours, their efforts were called off and the dead sailors' bodies were laid out in the ship's saloon, covered with a shared Union Jack.

Meanwhile, *Otter's* second lifeboat had been launched without the captain, Lieutenant Denis Mossman, who had been left behind in the confusion when he went below to confirm that no one was still on board. When the lifeboat returned to rescue him, it was so overcrowded that three sailors, Able Seaman Tom Guildford and Ordinary Seamen Ian O'Hara and John Slavin, decided to take their chances by joining others already clinging to a float. Unfortunately, O'Hara drowned shortly afterwards. After rescuing Mossman, the lifeboat made for the Polish vessel and arrived safely with fifteen passengers. Not having been in the freezing water, they were in much better shape than the men in Lifeboat No. 1 and were able to climb the rope ladder unassisted.

That left one more group in the frigid water, fifteen sailors bobbing about on the float. *Talisman* had joined the search for survivors and, coming as close as possible to the raft, heaved a lifeline to it. By then, eleven of its fifteen occupants had succumbed to the elements. Tom Guildford, from Bedford, was in the best shape among the remaining four and wrapped the line around each of his companions in turn, who were then hauled through the icy waters to the British sub.

When it was Guildford's turn to go, the raft had drifted so far away from the submarine that her crew could no longer throw the lifeline to him. As well, he was so exhausted by his efforts that he did not have the strength to paddle the raft any closer. The submarine's first lieutenant, K. W. M. Meyrick, tied the line around his left foot, jumped into the ocean from the conning tower, and swam twenty-seven metres to the raft. When he reached it, he tied the rope around Guildford's waist and hauled him back to the sub. Meyrick subsequently received the Royal Humane Society Bronze Medal for his bravery, but lost his life six months later in another submarine.

When *Otter* sank at 11:15, the frightening ordeal of her crew was finally over. Two officers and nineteen ratings had perished in the accident—five of them Nova Scotians—but twenty-two lived, thanks in large part to the heroism of Polish merchant seamen, British submariners, and Canadian sailors. The bravery of Guildford, Slavin, O'Hara, Gillis, Ordinary Telegraphist Alex Day, and Signalman Bill Hunter, was recognized by the award of a Mention-in-Dispatches "for gallantry and devotion to duty." O'Hara's, Gillis's, and Day's were posthumous. *Otter* was one of two RCN armed yachts lost during the war, out of a fleet of sixteen.

## DEATH ON CHRISTMAS EVE

On December 21, 1944, *U-806* under Kapitänleutnant Klaus Hornbostel attacked convoy HHX-327 off Halifax on her first war patrol. Coincidentally, the submarine skipper had been assistant gunnery officer in *Admiral Scheer* when the German surface raider attacked convoy HX-84 and sank *Jervis Bay* in November 1940. Two of the four torpedoes he fired at HHX-327 scored hits on the Liberty ship *Samtucky*. Although Hornbostel thought he had destroyed her, *Samtucky* was beached at Halifax and later repaired. Despite the increased state of alert he knew his attack would bring, the next day he was again off Chebucto Head, where he made an unsuccessful attack.

*The Bangor class minesweeper* HMCS Clayoquot *had been assigned to the Halifax Local Defence Force in October 1944.*

Meanwhile, the damage to *Samtucky* had been assessed as probably due to a mine, so authorities ordered the Halifax approaches swept. The frigate *Kirkland Lake* and the Bangor minesweepers *Transcona* and *Clayoquot* were selected for this task on December 22. Most of *Clayoquot*'s crew were on short Christmas leave at the time and were recalled immediately, including her seventh captain, Acting Lieutenant Commander Craig Campbell, who was at his home in Chester enjoying a fireside rum. The recall was not completely successful however, and Campbell was twenty-two men short. Replacements were drafted in from the manning depot.

Similarly, *Clayoquot* was far from ready to undertake minesweeping. She had been operating as a convoy escort for some time, and the majority of her sweeping gear had been removed, although she still carried the heavy minesweeping winch on her quarterdeck. At the French Cable Wharf in Dartmouth, additional minesweeping gear was quickly fitted.

On the morning of December 23, the tiny flotilla sailed out of the harbour, with *Kirkland Lake*'s captain as senior officer. It had been ordered to conduct an anti-submarine sweep through the areas that several ships would shortly sail, including convoy HB-139 headed for Boston and the troopship *Lady Rodney* sailing independently to St. John's. U-806 was about three kilometres from the Sambro Light Vessel when the three-ship escort group appeared on the scene. They were steaming line abreast to take up screening stations around the convoy, which consisted of the twelve Boston-bound merchantmen.

With at least one U-boat known to be in the area (in fact there were three), the three escorts were zigzagging as they approached the convoy, then broke formation on receipt of a flag signal from *Kirkland Lake* to take up their screening stations around it. At the same time, Hornbostel was only 365 metres off the port side of HB-139, selecting his targets. As *Clayoquot* turned to take up her new position, it took her directly towards the sub's track from astern. When Hornbostel saw this through his small attack periscope, he assumed he had been detected and the minesweeper was attacking him.

He quickly abandoned his attack on the convoy, fired a Gnat acoustic torpedo at *Clayoquot* as she steamed towards him, and dove to fifty metres. Sixty-nine seconds later—at 11:40—the torpedo struck the minesweeper's stern, and the ship quickly listed to starboard. A second explosion followed almost immediately, as some of the depth charges went off. This second-ary explosion blew twelve metres of the stern into a vertical position and scattered parts of the minesweeping gear over the forecastle. Simultaneously, pieces of depth charges rained down on the bridge and through the galley skylight onto the cook's stove. Dense clouds of smoke and steam rose into the air, obscuring Campbell's view from the bridge.

Two officers and three ratings were killed instantly in the explosion, but fortunately most of the ship's company were forward for their daily grog issue and escaped injury. Two other officers were trapped in the after officers' cabin and as *Clayoquot* settled lower in the water they screamed through a scuttle for help or an axe to chop themselves free. But the axes were already underwater and nothing could be done to save them. One of the

*Survivors of* HMCS Clayoquot, *which was torpedoed by the German submarine* U-806, *are rescued by the corvette* HMCS Fennel *off Halifax, Christmas Eve, 1944.*

*HMCS Clayoquot's captain, Lieutenant Commander Craig Campbell, looks directly at the camera in the lower left of the photograph, as his sailors are taken aboard the corvette HMCS Fennel, off Halifax, December 24, 1944.*

minesweeper's eight-metre whalers was cut loose from the starboard side as it reached the water, allowing several sailors to get away. As the ship rolled farther to starboard, Campbell ordered "Abandon ship!" and his men jumped into the frigid December water. Within ten minutes, *Clayoquot* turned turtle and sank, stern first.

Everything happened so quickly that there had not been time to remove the primers from the emergency depth charges on the stern and they went off as *Clayoquot* went down. Fortunately, the crewmen were wearing newly developed life jackets with a protective crotch piece, which resulted in fewer critical injuries, although the men in the water were hurt and a stoker died. In *The Canadian Naval Chronicle 1939–1945* by Robert Darlington and Fraser McKee, Campbell described it as feeling like being lifted up and "then dropped onto a concrete slab."

*Clayoquot's* companions and the frigate *Fennel*, which had been escorting another convoy out of Halifax, witnessed the torpedoing. *Transcona* immediately streamed her CAT (Canadian Anti-Acoustic Torpedo) gear—a noisemaking device towed a safe distance astern to draw torpedoes away from a ship's propellers—and headed towards the sinking minesweeper to rescue survivors. As she approached, one of the freighters signalled she had seen a sub on the surface, so *Transcona* sailed on and dropped off four Carley floats as she steamed by the survivors. Within ten minutes her CAT exploded another torpedo fired by *u-806*.

As *Kirkland Lake* searched for the U-boat, *Fennel* moved to pick up survivors in the icy water. Knowing there were several ships available to rescue them, the sailors on the rafts and in the water kept their spirits up by singing. *The Canadian Naval Chronicle* notes that one even yelled out a spoof news announcement: "Flash! Canadian Minesweeper Destroys German Torpedo!" In about forty minutes, all seventy-six men in the water were rescued. Eight others—four officers and four ratings—died in the sinking.

As the escorts searched for *u-806*, Hornbostel dove to sixty metres, passed under the convoy, and at 1:10 settled on the bottom in sixty-eight metres of water. Other ships arrived from Halifax and soon a flotilla of twenty-one frigates, corvettes, minesweepers, motor torpedo boats, and trawlers were scouring the area. They searched until December 26 without success. After eleven hours on the bottom, Hornbostel made his way slowly south for another ten hours and remained undetected.

A Board of Inquiry on December 26 did not assign any blame for *Clayoquot*'s sinking and made only two minor recommendations for future anti-submarine operations. *Fennel*'s captain received a Mention-in-Dispatches, along with one of his officers and two of *Clayoquot*'s sailors who had helped their shipmates in the water. *u-806* survived the war, surrendered at Wilhelmshaven, and was later scrapped. Klaus Hornbostel and Craig Campbell, who both continued to serve after the war, began to correspond. They met on two occasions, put their adversarial past behind them, and became friends.

## THE LAST SINKING

IN THE EARLY MORNING of April 16, 1945, the Bangor minesweeper HMCS *Esquimalt* was on a routine anti-submarine patrol in the approaches to Halifax Harbour under Lieutenant Robert Macmillan, who had earlier won both the Distinguished Service Cross and Bar in the Mediterranean. *Esquimalt* was scheduled to meet another minesweeper, HMCS *Sarnia*, which was patrolling another sector, at 8:00 AM. The morning was relatively calm and clear, and the crew had switched off their old radar, relying on asdic to detect any U-boats that might be in the area. To compound her mistakes, *Esquimalt* neither zigzagged nor deployed her CAT.

At 6:20, close to the Sambro Light Vessel, *u-190* heard *Esquimalt*'s pinging. Her captain, Oberleutnant zur See Hans-Edwin Reith, who had been lying in wait for just such a target, took a quick glance through his periscope, thought he was under attack, and fired off a Gnat torpedo. It quickly found its mark, so fast in fact that the asdic operator reported nothing, no radio message went out, and not even a flare was fired. *Esquimalt* went down in four minutes. Two of her six Carley float releases jammed, possibly because of poor maintenance. Reith escaped in the same way Hornbostel had.

Petty Officer Terrence Manuel had just come off watch at the depth-charge throwers and was stretched out in his hammock in his shorts, hoping to catch forty winks.

TOP *The Bangor class minesweeper* HMCS Esquimalt *in St. Margaret's Bay, May 1944.*
BOTTOM *Minesweepers were small, crowded vessels, as shown by the messdeck of this unidentified minesweeper at Halifax, March 17, 1944.*

Miraculously, Manuel got out and swam to a floating kit bag, where he helped a fellow sailor cling to it. As the bag slowly sank, Petty Officer Carl Jacques spotted them from a Carley float. Jacques knew Manuel could not swim, so he swam over to the two and got them back to the float. But the cold water and the strenuous effort were too much; Jacques died while Manuel lived.

Most of the others were as lightly dressed as Manuel—the navigating officer was in shirt and shorts, while the chief bosun's mate was incongruously wearing red pyjamas. Most were without life jackets. Despite the ice-cold ducking they had received, the sailors were not too worried. The sea was calm, the Sambro Light Vessel close, the shore not far off, and it was brightening as the sun came up.

But the light vessel crew sent out no signal; perhaps they were asleep. Two minesweepers approached at nine o'clock, causing the survivors to wave and shout. Unbelievably, the vessels passed within three kilometres and sailed on; their lookouts and officers of the watch were certainly not paying attention. Aircraft flew over, but later their crews admitted they thought the yellow Carley floats were local fishermen. Spirits shattered, shivering from the icy water, several of the sailors withdrew into a trance and simply drifted off into

*Survivors of the minesweeper* HMCS Esquimalt, *which was torpedoed by the German submarine* U-190 *on April 16, 1945, await rescue on a float off Halifax. Several of them wear only the clothes in which they were sleeping when the torpedo struck.*

*Survivors of the minesweeper* HMCS Esquimalt *disembark from the rescue minesweeper* HMCS Sarnia *at Halifax, April 16, 1945.*

death. Seven hours later, *Sarnia*, delayed by her own earlier anti-submarine attacks, stumbled upon the survivors and sent in the first word of the torpedoing. By then, forty-four of *Esquimalt*'s seventy-one-man crew had succumbed to the cold—the RCN's last combat deaths in the unforgiving North Atlantic.

*The merchant ship SS* Marquesa *undergoes repairs in Halifax's floating drydock, 1942.*

## CHAPTER 6

# THE SAILORS WHO SAVED THE CITY

### A CLEAR AND PRESENT DANGER

WITH SO MANY MERCHANT SHIPS carrying explosive cargoes and warships loaded with ammunition entering and leaving the port of Halifax during the war, residents remained fearful of a repeat of the disastrous explosion of a generation earlier. On a couple of occasions there were some near disasters, but in each case a catastrophe was averted. It was not until shortly after the war ended that the explosion everyone dreaded actually occurred.

The danger was not only that ammunition or other explosives on a merchant vessel or warship could blow up, but also that a ship carrying a dangerous cargo would be torpedoed or hit a mine at the harbour entrance. There were several close calls. In broad daylight on

February 22, 1942, *u-96* torpedoed the 12,400-ton British tanker *Kars* off Ketch Harbour, some twenty-two kilometres southwest of Sambro Island. The torpedo punched a hole in one of the ship's storage tanks, igniting the fuel inside and allowing it to flow out.

Soon the ship was surrounded by a field of burning gasoline, which set the vessel afire. Many of her crew were trapped aboard, while others died in the flaming fuel field as they tried to get away. Forty-six seamen of forty-seven burned to death. The tanker was taken in tow and beached on Ives Point on McNabs Island, where she continued to burn and smoulder for days, an all-too-visible reminder of the dangers faced daily by merchant ships and their crews.

## A NEAR RUN THING

ONE OF THE HARBOUR'S most spectacular incidents began at 9:50 PM on April 9, 1942. The 7,000-ton American cargo ship SS *Trongate*, moored off the Halifax ferry terminal north of Georges Island, was waiting to join a convoy to Britain when she flashed a frantic signal from an Aldis lamp: "Require immediate assistance. Fire below decks."

In her holds, *Trongate* carried 1,981 drums of highly flammable toluene (an organic compound represented by the second "T" in TNT), as well as thirty cases of filled shells, 10,474 cases of filled cartridges, and 3,506 boxes of small arms ammunition. An explosion would have been disastrous, as the port was crammed with more than two hundred ships—including packed troopships—the second largest number of the entire war, totalling nearly 2,000,000 tons. If she exploded, the ship's position in the harbour would also ensure there was extensive damage to the port's important infrastructure, as well as to downtown Halifax and Dartmouth.

*Trongate* had been in Halifax since the previous November undergoing repairs. During that time, her crew earned an unenviable reputation. According to H. B. Jefferson, the regional censor of publications, they were the "toughest, 'fightingest' crew that ever entered Halifax Harbour." On one occasion, when a *Trongate* sailor was thrown out of a seaman's hostel, he bit a policemen's finger, which caused blood poisoning. He then went to a dance where he got into a fight that resulted in his jaw being broken. After receiving treatment in hospital, he returned to the same dance hall the next evening, ready to take on his previous night's adversary.

Once the fire on *Trongate* was reported, the fireboat *Rouille* and a number of tugs quickly arrived on the scene and poured water into the ship. Flames were not yet visible above deck when at ten o'clock *Trongate* again flashed her original signal and added "I have TNT aboard." To the few people watching from the shore at that hour, nothing seemed particularly out of the ordinary and there was no panic.

Other signals flashed during the next two hours, alerting necessary parties that the fire was out of control and the captain intended to send the crew ashore and scuttle his ship.

*A damaged Canadian Merchant Navy ship at Halifax, one of a number built in Canada during the Second World War and named after Canadian parks. Similar to the better-known American Liberty ships, in addition to their regular civilian crew, they carried about half a dozen naval gunners aboard for defence and were known as* DEMS—*Defensively Equipped Merchant Ships. When in convoy torpedo nets were lowered over the side.*

*Interested spectators view the new Halifax fireboat* Rouille, *docked at Purdy's Wharf, July 10, 1941. Nine months later* Rouille *valiantly fought the fire aboard the ammunition-laden American cargo ship* ss Trongate *until* hmcs Chedabucto *arrived to sink her.*

This was followed with a signal from the dockyard indicating that a naval explosives party was on the way, and that the minesweeper "*Chedabucto* will stand by to sink by gunfire if necessary."

## *CHEDABUCTO* IN ACTION

INITIALLY IT WAS THOUGHT that gunners manning the high-calibre guns of the harbour forts might be able to sink *Trongate*. This option was quickly dismissed when gunnery experts pointed out that large-calibre shells could ricochet off the water and cause extensive property damage and personal injury—or even death—in Dartmouth.

When *Chedabucto*, a Bangor class minesweeper, arrived about 2:45 AM, the fireboat and tugs left the scene. As the minesweeper's searchlight played across *Trongate*, flames burst from her superstructure near the funnel; the fire was getting worse. Sailors trained the searchlight on the precise waterline of the ship and left it there. It was crucial that any shells fired hit the waterline; any higher would not allow water to enter the hull, while lower could result in a ricochet, with potentially dangerous results.

*Chedabucto*'s crew fired a round of 4-inch practice shot—ammunition filled with sand instead of explosives—into *Trongate*'s hull at the waterline. Despite the risk of certain death if the ship exploded, the minesweeper's courageous eighty or so sailors stayed at

*HMCS* Chedabucto *calmly and deliberately sank* Trongate *to prevent her ammunition from exploding on April 10, 1942.*

their stations, guiding their vessel methodically around the burning ship; refocussing the searchlight each time they stopped to fire another round. The booming of *Chedabucto's* gun attracted the curious and the concerned, but telephone operators had been warned about what was happening and calmed people by telling them that "a burning ship is being sunk by gunfire and there is no danger."

The blazing vessel presented a spectacular scene, especially when various types of ammunition exploded and sent sparks, flames, and even gold and red signal rockets arcing skywards, accompanied by the sound of incessant gunfire as small-arms ammunition cooked off. Experienced sailors likened it to a night engagement at sea. After *Chedabucto* had fired about twenty-five rounds into *Trongate*, the stricken ship began to settle lower and lower into the water. At 3:25 AM she turned slightly on her side and went down in twenty-three metres of water.

Later that morning, despite the excellent work of *Chedabucto's* crew and the extreme care they had taken in laying their gun, it was discovered that one round had either missed its target or gone clean through the ship and ricocheted onto the Dartmouth shore, where it went through the roof of a business and landed inside. When one of the women who worked in the building came in that morning, she found the shell sitting beside her desk as if someone had gently placed it there.

*Workmen adjust a diver's helmet before salvage begins on the cargo of a sunken ship in an "east coast port," July 1943. By repairing damaged ships and salvaging sunken cargo, the Department of Munitions and Supply saved important tonnage and millions of dollars worth of war supplies.*

*Chedabucto* did not survive the war. On the night of October 21, 1943, she collided with the cable vessel *Lord Kelvin* in the St. Lawrence River, fifty kilometres from Rimouski, Quebec, with the loss of her engineering officer. She was subsequently towed inshore and grounded on a mud flat. Due to the extremely soft bottom and strong current, salvage was not possible.

*Trongate* was salvaged, but the impression of her hull remains on the harbour floor today. Known as the "Trongate Depression," it is 125 metres long and surrounded by berms—the highest two metres above the seabed—where the weight of the ship squished soft mud up the sides of the hull as she settled on the bottom.

# ALCOHOL AND POKER

ABOUT EIGHTEEN MONTHS LATER, Halifax had another brush with a dangerous situation, one that also had the potential for a second Halifax Explosion. The hero of the moment this time was Commander Owen Connor Struan Robertson, a giant of a man, better known as "Long Robbie" to his contemporaries and "Big Robbie" to his juniors because of his two-metre height. Robertson, a descendant of generations of seamen, was a sailor's sailor with a record of service in both merchant vessels and warships during peace- and wartime stretching back to 1915, when he was only eight years old.

Robertson joined the Royal Canadian Naval Reserve in 1931 while serving on the Lady Boats, the fleet of small, cargo-passenger liners sailing between the Maritimes and the West Indies. During the Second World War, he was both Commander of His Majesty's Canadian Dockyard and King's Harbour Master in Halifax, where his heroism twice prevented a repeat of the devastating Halifax Explosion of 1917. Several years later, Robertson recorded his experiences in volume three of *Salty Dips*, published by the Ottawa branch of the Naval Officers' Association of Canada.

On the first occasion, the 10,000-ton American freighter ss *Volunteer* was anchored in Bedford Basin on the evening of November 2, 1943, laden with five hundred tons of small arms ammunition, eighteen hundred tons of heavy howitzer shells, two thousand barrels of highly combustible magnesium powder, a large number of depth charges, a smaller amount of dynamite and, curiously, several large bales of tobacco. Eighty other ships were anchored along with her, awaiting the departure of their convoy.

*Volunteer*'s green wartime crew was confined on board to protect her cargo and was not allowed to go ashore. Bored, and with nothing better to do, a number of the ship's officers decided to play poker—and drink. The poker game progressed through the night, and so did the drinking. The captain, chief engineer, chief officer, and second engineer were soon intoxicated. Dangerous cargo, raw crew, and drunken officers: ingredients for a disaster. It was not long coming.

At about 5:15 the next morning, an inexperienced stoker attempted to fire up one of the two boilers using the wrong procedure, setting the boiler room on fire. As the stoker fled to safety, the second mate, long overdue for relief by the chief mate, reported the fire to the master. He received no reaction from him or any of the other officers, who merely continued their drunken poker game. Confusion reigned as the fire spread and all attempts by the leaderless crew to fight it proved ineffectual.

Eventually someone succeeded in getting an sos sent out by wireless (initially on the wrong frequency) and signal lamp (initially in the wrong direction). After some difficulty, a local naval signal station succeeded in pinpointing *Volunteer*'s location. It notified the Naval Control Service, which dispatched a boat to determine the problem. About ten minutes before the navy vessel arrived, *Volunteer*'s crew took to the ship's

*The fireboat* Rouille *in action.* Rouille *helped keep the fire aboard the American freighter ss* Volunteer *under control until the ammunition-laden ship could be beached at Maugers Beach.*

boats and headed for shore, in an action reminiscent of *Mont Blanc*'s crew a quarter of a century earlier.

Robertson, whose responsibilities included the safety of all vessels in port, was contacted about 7:05 AM and rushed to his launch, waiting with six firefighters aboard. Meanwhile, the fire tug *Rouille* from the Halifax Fire Department had come alongside *Volunteer* and begun pumping foam into the blazing boiler room.

## VOLUNTEERS ON *VOLUNTEER*

ROBERTSON ARRIVED ON THE SCENE at the same time as the National Harbours Board fireboat *James Battle* and immediately boarded *Volunteer* to assess the situation, along with the navy's fire marshal and the board's fire captain. As they searched the burning ship, they soon discovered the drunken poker game but could not get any sense out of the ship's officers. Robertson was now in a quandary; he had no authority over the master of a foreign merchant ship, but if he did not do something, and quickly, the ship and her cargo might soon be lost, or far worse.

As similarities with the Halifax Explosion crossed his mind, the sounds of bullets going off told him the fire had reached the small-arms ammunition stored below. He had to act immediately. Robertson arranged for the United States naval observer in Halifax to come aboard and formally relieve *Volunteer*'s captain of his command, then set about assessing the extent of the fire. It was worse than he expected.

Although foam had extinguished the fire in the boiler room, cargo was burning in No. 3 Hold, threatening to blow up and spread the flames. The most immediate danger came from eight barrels of magnesium; if they blew up they could destroy the whole ship. Without hesitating, Robertson entered the hold, followed by a couple of firefighters. They crawled over the top of the cargo towards the magnesium as smoke from burning tobacco and cordite engulfed them and small-arms rounds kept popping off all around them.

They found the magnesium drums, fortunately separated from each other by tobacco bales. Robertson resorted to a desperate ploy to save the ship. He had a crew of dockyard welders cut large holes in the deck above the magnesium, intending to blow the drums up one by one to vent the explosions through the holes and prevent a rupture of the bulkhead with No. 2 Hold.

While the welders worked, firefighters stacked more tobacco bales around the magnesium to protect them. After about an hour's heavy work this was finished, and Robertson fired into each barrel with a rifle from behind a row of bales. It worked. The drums went off one by one, flames roaring out through the holes in the deck above them; however, when two drums unexpectedly went off together, the blast tossed Robertson and other firefighters about like rag dolls.

Some were knocked out, including Robertson, while others were merely winded. One was blown right out of the hold and later died in hospital from severe injuries and gassing. Those on deck quickly pulled the others from the hold and revived the unconscious ones; Robertson woke up as seawater was poured on his face. Although fires still burned below decks, and flame and smoke billowed into the sky above the ship, the blaze was eventually brought under control.

The civilian crew of the fireboat *James Battle* now decided the area was too dangerous for them and announced they were leaving. Dishevelled, shaken, staggering, covered in black soot, blood trickling down his face, Robertson grabbed the rifle and yelled, "The first man who touches a line is *dead!*" It worked. By then, Lieutenant Commander Ted Watt had come aboard with his Naval Boarding Party and, just to be sure, one of his men was stationed on a wing of the bridge to keep an eye on things—while holding a rifle.

Robertson convened a quick council of war to consider the options: sinking *Volunteer* where she was or moving her to the far side of Bedford Basin and sinking her there. Both had their disadvantages, primarily the loss of the vessel and her much-needed wartime cargo. There was a third option, a dangerous one that would save the ship and her cargo, but it depended on keeping the fire under control until the ship could reach the beaching point on McNabs Island.

It meant taking the ship through the Narrows—where the *Mont Blanc* had exploded—and passing the most heavily populated parts of both sides of the harbour. But it also meant *Volunteer* could be scuttled with her main decks above water, making her eventual salvage much easier. The decision was made to try for Maugers Beach; a harbour pilot and tugs were requested. In the meantime, Robertson climbed down into smoke-filled No. 2 Hold, where the occasional bullet zinged passed him. Fortunately, it appeared as if the hoses could keep the flames under control long enough to prevent them from reaching the howitzer ammunition in the lower hold.

When the two tugs arrived, the anchor cable was cut with an oxyacetylene torch and they began towing *Volunteer* with *Rouille* tied alongside, her hoses playing water into No. 3 Hold. At about 3:00 PM, as the little flotilla sailed through the Narrows and into the inner harbour on their way to McNabs Island, Haligonians were spared the knowledge of

*Cases of salvaged goods are hoisted from a sunken freighter in an "east coast port," July 1943.*

the drama that was unfolding a short distance away. About twenty minutes after the ship began to make its way down the harbour, the captain appeared on the bridge, "very, very drunk and, grabbing a megaphone, shouted at the fo'c'sle head, with nobody on it, 'Heave up the anchor!'" Forty-five minutes later, the two tugs manoeuvred the burning vessel over a spot at Maugers Beach where she could be safely beached with her main deck slightly above the water. The seacocks were opened and the ship settled onto the gravel bottom, steam hissing as seawater put out the remaining fires.

The ship and most of her cargo were salvaged, and a mere three weeks later, *Volunteer* sailed for England in convoy, with a new captain and crew. Robertson's bravery and leadership won him the George Medal—slightly below the Victoria Cross—awarded for valour not in the face of the enemy. He was one of only seventy-six Canadians ever to attain this honour, his citation referring to "a second Halifax Explosion averted."

## BEDFORD MAGAZINE

EVENTUALLY THE BIG EXPLOSION that everyone dreaded happened, but it was not during the war. Two months after the end of the war in Europe and the disruptive V-E Day riots (chapter 7), a second Halifax Explosion did occur, when fires and blasts rocked the Bedford Magazine. The magazine, whose eight-hundred-metre width stretched along five kilometres of the basin's eastern shore, had been built in 1927 for use by the navy, army, and air force, replacing older, smaller ones closer to the city. The new depot consisted of a series of well-ventilated, small brick buildings. Each one was surrounded by a berm of earth and concrete, designed to contain any accidental blast and force it upwards and away from its neighbours.

Prior to the war, the magazine could not even meet the ammunition storage needs of the RCN and additional funds had been allocated for its expansion. This did not happen until after the war started however, and by mid-1943 more than $1,300,000 had been spent on improving the facility, which by then was used exclusively by the navy. Despite this expansion, the Bedford Magazine continued to be severely overused, and it was impossible to fully comply with all safety regulations. When the war in Europe ended in May 1945, the situation became far worse. The explosion that had been "narrowly averted" so many times during the war was about to happen.

Masses of ammunition were stacked on the wharf from returning warships prior to their decommissioning. Political pressure was applied from the Liberal government to unload the ships—normally a slow process—as rapidly as possible to get their mostly reservist crews home. Many safety regulations were ignored in the name of expediency. In particular, while a jetty should only have been stacked with one ship's ammunition, often the ammunition from three ships was there at the same time, in piles up to two metres high.

# THE SECOND HALIFAX EXPLOSION

THE MIDDLE WEEK OF JULY brought a heat wave to Halifax, leaving brush, grass, and leaves at the Bedford Magazine and elsewhere highly flammable. About 6:30 PM on July 18, a fire broke out in a barge tied up at the naval magazine's South Jetty, widely believed to be caused by a pyrotechnic flare that leaked and then burst into flame. One of the naval guards, Able Seaman Henry Craig spotted the fire and yelled to a mate, "I'm going down to see if I can put it out." He had just reached the end of the jetty when the whole structure blew up, flinging him about 180 metres inland. Craig's body was not found until three days later. The fire quickly spread and set off a number of explosions that threatened to blow up the rest of the ammunition stored there, with the potential for taking a good part of the city with it.

Long Robbie Robertson had just sat down to have dinner with his wife in the Nova Scotian Hotel, when "there was a *bang* and all of the dust came out of the ventilators." He rushed to a top-floor room overlooking the harbour and saw "a mushroom cloud *over the magazine!*" Robertson headed for the dock, where his boat was already waiting to take him across the harbour to the magazine. He intended to land at the South Jetty, but when he got there "the jetty had disappeared," so he landed at the North Jetty and went ashore to assess the situation. It was not good.

*Exploding ammunition arcs skyward from the Bedford ammunition magazine fire, July 18, 1945, silhouetting the Halifax skyline.*

"The south end had gone. The buildings were gone. The water tower had come down with one of the first explosions." About a third to a half of the older part of the dump—perhaps 160 hectares—was already in ruins. By virtue of his job at the time of the explosion, Robertson was put in charge of the efforts of all firefighters: military and civilian, permanent and volunteer. Although the daytime workers had already gone home, about two hundred volunteered to come back.

Robertson feared the worst and recommended the evacuation of all Halifax residents who lived along the Bedford Highway or north of North Street (later extended to Quinpool Road) as a safety precaution. Thousands of residents of north-end Halifax, as well as Dartmouth, were evacuated and several civilian and naval ships weighed anchor and moved out of range. Those that did not have enough time to get up steam, including vessels undergoing repairs at the shipyards, were pushed out of the way by tugs or taken in tow by other ships. No one wanted to risk a repetition of the 1917 explosion.

After Robertson arrived at the site, a reinforced concrete building he was standing near suddenly blew up, flinging him into a pond. With the magazine's water main destroyed in the first blast, water had to be pumped in from static water tanks and a nearby stream by the firefighters, who eventually succeeded in flooding the newer magazines to prevent further explosions.

As they battled the tenacious fire, exploding shells and bullets frequently drove Robertson's firefighting teams to the ground and several got hit, "but all they did was make you black and blue." Shells up to 4-inch would separate, with the bullet going one way and

*The Bedford Magazine explosion of July 18, 1945, devastated several buildings and large areas of the ammunition depot.*

*Explosions at the Bedford ammunition magazine continued throughout the night of July 18, 1945.*

the shell casing the other. "Some of the smaller ones were going so slowly that you could catch a 20-millimetre round in your hand—but not gracefully."

The heat, heavy work, and lack of water soon dehydrated Robertson and his men—plus they had no food. He radioed headquarters for something to be sent out for his hungry workers. "What we would have welcomed was lettuce and ice cream—maybe sandwiches—but good old Central Victualling Depot sent us a slab of beef and a sack of raw potatoes." Robertson was furious and after twenty-four hours without sleep more than a little irritable. He got on the radio again, this time on an open channel, cursed whoever was in charge of the depot and threatened to "have this guy's balls for a necktie." Ice cream and sandwiches soon arrived.

After two nerve-racking days of heroic efforts, Robertson again led his men to success. Damage in Halifax was largely limited to shattered windows, broken plaster, downed power lines, and cracked foundations. Miraculously, Craig was the only fatality. The courageous firefighting of sailors did much to dispel the lingering resentment among Haligonians as a result of the earlier V-E Day riots. And Long Robbie, the man who twice saved Halifax from a potentially disastrous repeat of the 1917 explosion, was simply doing his job.

*Sailors and civilians—plus a couple of soldiers—line up for a movie at the Orpheus Theatre next to the Green Lantern Restaurant on Barrington Street, 1941.*

CHAPTER 7

# REACHING THE BOILING POINT

### LIFE IN "AN EAST COAST PORT"

THROUGHOUT THE SECOND WORLD WAR, Canadian newspapers often mentioned "an East Coast Port" in their articles, ostensibly as a security measure. While it could have referred to any one of several locations, it almost always meant Halifax. Sailors scornfully referred to the city by another name—"Slackers"—a euphemism that conjured up those who were avoiding the war, both civilian and naval. Conflict had once again thrust Halifax and its large, deep, protected harbour on the edge of major North Atlantic sea lanes into the spotlight. It was a spotlight many Haligonians would rather have avoided.

During the war, Halifax quickly became overcrowded with tens of thousands of military and naval personnel, as well as merchant seamen, civilian workers, and their families. The population rose by 60 per cent, from 78,000 to 124,000. Newcomers competed with locals for food and other commodities, accommodation, and public and private services. All remained in short supply throughout the war and never did meet the needs of the influx of people. Despite clearly being the Canadian city hardest hit by the war, the federal government irrationally refused to recognize Halifax's unique status and steadfastly—some might say stupidly—maintained that all cities in the country were equally affected.

Many service personnel resented the overcrowding in the city, in both civilian and military accommodation. Unscrupulous landlords overcharged for the tiniest of substandard living space, which frequently saw shared toilet, ablution, and cooking facilities—if there were any at all. The RCN's facilities were not always better. Under the pressure of an ever-increasing number of Canadian and British sailors who required accommodation in Halifax, the navy soon outgrew its original dockyard along the waterfront, a narrow strip about a kilometre long and 150 metres wide.

*Overcrowding in the dockyard led the navy to take over King's College for reserve officer training in 1942 and commission it as HMCS Kings.*

To accommodate additional sailors, the navy took over the Industrial Building at the Exhibition Grounds from the army and commissioned it as HMCS *Stadacona II* in 1940, while the dockyard became known as *Stadacona I*. Numbers of sailors soon exceeded the space available however, and Wellington Barracks was taken over from the army in 1941. It was renamed Nelson Barracks (later *Stadacona*) and quickly had three new blocks added to it. In 1942, administration of all naval schools in the city was placed under a newly commissioned training establishment, HMCS *Cornwallis*, which moved to the shores of the Annapolis Basin in 1943. Finally, the RCN obtained the RCAF's Windsor Park in 1944 and commissioned it as HMCS *Peregrine*; a depot to control the drafting and advancement of ratings. But crowding persisted.

During the early years of the war, sailors were welcomed and generally shown unrivalled hospitality. Initially, local branches of various national volunteer service groups, such as the Salvation Army, Red Cross, Canadian Legion, YMCA, and Knights of Columbus, had set up canteens where service personnel could relax and get a light meal. Added to these were similar facilities established by several churches and strictly local organizations. But these were soon overwhelmed as more and more men in uniform poured into the city, and life for a sailor in Halifax became an unpleasant experience.

Service personnel believed they were ignored by the vast majority of Haligonians, who appeared to regard them as little more than an opportunity to make money by overcharging

*The North End Services Canteen, February 1941, was established by concerned Haligonians. At its peak, it served over a thousand meals a day to service personnel.*

for substandard accommodation, meals, and entertainment. They also detested the terrible service and—perhaps most of all—antiquated liquor laws.

According to Professor Archibald MacMechan of Dalhousie University, Nova Scotia's great Victorian-Edwardian man of letters, "When a sailor makes a port after a voyage, two things he must have. One of them is a drink." Sub-Lieutenant "Yogi" Jensen of Calgary personally experienced Halifax's rigid control of alcohol when he passed through the city on his way home from Britain in the fall of 1941, as he recorded in *Tin Hats, Oilskins, and Sea Boots: A Naval Journey, 1938–1945.* Looking for a quiet place downtown to have a drink, to his amazement he found none. "Having just come from the British Isles where pubs were part of every community, we learned it was not possible to buy an alcoholic drink of any kind in any public place in Nova Scotia." This was quickly contrasted with the wardroom at Admiralty House, where "liquor was much in evidence. In fact," he noted, "I have never before seen such devoted attention to the subject."

Jensen explored Halifax during the few days he spent there, and his impressions were not good. His experience of Canadian cities had been largely limited to Calgary and Vancouver, which he thought compared favourably to the cities and towns he had seen in Britain. Nothing had prepared him for Halifax. "The buildings for the most part were

*Sailing on the Northwest Arm was a popular activity for many off-duty service personnel in Halifax during the Second World War.*

*Mostly naval personnel and their partners crowd this dance floor in wartime Halifax.*

run down, and the streets were dirty with newspapers and garbage blowing about. Houses were unpainted and some of the streets were still not paved." Even the large Victorian mansions of the South End needed painting. Apparently the owners believed that "painting a house increased the taxes." On Market Street below Citadel Hill, Jensen saw houses that he judged to be worse than ones he had seen in West Africa.

In *An East Coast Port*, Graham Metson recorded the stories of several military and civilian residents of the city. One of them, Hal Brown, would change from his uniform into civvies on weekends to go to the Dingle to rent a rowboat. The boats were reasonably priced, as opposed to the canteen, which was "inadequate and overpriced." He described the canteen's thirty-five-cent ham sandwich, "which wasn't ham at all but a thin slice of bologna, a scraping of mustard, no butter, the bread so thin you could read a paper through it." At the same time the Jewish Congress Canteen offered a salami sandwich with three layers of meat for ten or fifteen cents. "Prices for pop and coffee were also outrageous," he recalled, "and this was true nearly all over the city."

Metson noted that many working civilians shared the sailors' opinion of the port city. One dock worker said that "Halifax was dreary, dismal and boring. You could feel the tension growing and the anger." Marjorie Whitelaw, who came to Halifax from Montreal during the early days of the war and worked in the Children's Hospital, called the city "exciting, terrible, heartrending, lively." At the hospital, she observed first-hand a litany of social pressures that affected Halifax during the war: "children abandoned in the hospital because their mothers had to work [and] impossible housing conditions."

In *Halifax, Warden of the North*, Thomas H. Raddall made a few pithy comments on a sailor's other need besides drink. By the time the Second World War began, many of Halifax's surviving brothels had adjusted to the age of the car and relocated outside the city, where there were no bothersome police. With the influx of servicemen during the war, "madams and harlots flocked to the city by rail and air" and plied their trade in small brothels on the outskirts. Others sought a more glamorous life inside the city and "for six years the port was a courtesan's paradise far surpassing the days of 1918." Only now it was much more discreet—"and dainty." Prostitutes "exacted a high price for [their] favours, and bestowed them in snug flats and apartments." As a result, the prostitute of 1942, "wore a fur coat and a smart dress, travelled in taxicabs, patronized the best shops and restaurants, [and] let herself be seen at the best dances."

Despite the influx of "new" prostitutes, old-style brothels still flourished in the city. Halifax's most popular one was run by Germaine Pelletier in a red brick house at 51 Hollis Street, across from Government House, the official residence of the lieutenant-governor. A long line of men—in and out of uniform—could often be seen waiting outside the house. As the war ground on, the line began to form around noon and often stretched as far south as the Nova Scotian Hotel.

## AJAX CLUB

SEVERAL RESIDENTS TRIED TO IMPROVE the lot of sailors stationed in or passing through Halifax by making their stay as pleasant as possible under the circumstances. With facilities so limited, many citizens opened their homes to sailors. Once a seaman was assigned to a ship, he often found himself on a list for an open house. "Every time that ship came back to port they'd beat it to the phone," Whitelaw remembered, hoping for an invitation.

One of the city's most successful experiments in accomplishing this—at least for a time—was the Ajax Club. Janet "Dolly" McEuan, the wife of a naval officer, organized a group of citizens interested in providing servicemen a place to go for a quiet drink. They bought a large, vacant mansion at the corner of Tobin and Queen streets and opened it as the Ajax Club in December 1940. The club was an instant success. Servicemen could buy a meal or enjoy a beer, read, write letters, or just relax in an extremely pleasant setting. The club's proponents had given their endeavour plenty of thought and got the support of both the Liquor Commission and the Fort Massey United Church, across the street from the club. But it appears that some people simply could not stand the idea of a serviceman enjoying a well-earned beer, and in 1940s Nova Scotia, the powers of temperance and prohibition advocates were great.

*A corner of the ratings' lounge in the Ajax Club, Halifax.*

In the end, by strongly pressuring politicians and others, the Fort Massey Church—under a new minister—succeeded in persuading the Liquor Commission not to renew the club's beer licence. The club closed in February 1942, but not before its plight garnered support from across the country. Haligonians were exposed on the national stage as small-minded, petty, intolerant country bumpkins; however, even worse was to follow.

## THE V-E DAY RIOTS

AS THE END OF THE WAR approached, everybody—military and civilian alike—was fed up with the condition and range of facilities in the port city. According to one Wren, "The city was just plain overcrowded, and it made for a lot of tension." Although military and civilian authorities tried to make plans for celebrations in anticipation of the war's end, many of them were half-hearted. When Rear Admiral Leonard Murray—his attention understandably focussed on the U-boats' final offensive in Canadian waters—advised his subordinate commanders in February 1945 to make plans for the event, Captain Harold Balfour, in charge of the naval barracks, announced that he would declare an "Open Gangway" and "Sunday Routine," which meant that anyone except those on essential duties could leave the barracks.

Before the event, Mayor Allan Butler asked the area's eleven movie houses to remain open on V-E Day. They refused, even placing an ad in the newspapers to announce the

*Rear Admiral Leonard Murray, 1942, became the only Canadian to command an independent theatre of war—Canadian Northwest Atlantic—during the Second World War. Rightly or wrongly, he would carry much of the blame for the V-E Day riots.*

fact. Of the fifty-five restaurants in the city, only sixteen remained open on May 7, while on V-E Day itself forty-six were closed all day and most of the rest closed before 4:00 PM. All liquor stores were closed, although *Stadacona's* wet canteen opened briefly. Bootlegged liquor was available until supplies ran out, with cheap rye going for an exorbitant fifteen dollars a bottle. On the day when service personnel should have been able to celebrate their hard-earned victory over the tough enemy they had fought for the previous six years, there were no movies to watch, no restaurants in which to eat, and no alcohol to drink.

Coupled with pent-up resentment among naval personnel in particular over the lack of services and other shortcomings, the widespread closures were a recipe for disaster. Reactions boiled over when the news that the war had ended leaked out prematurely at 10:30 on the morning of May 7. People left work and took to the streets to celebrate. In the North End, sailors managed to stop a streetcar outside *Stadacona* and smash its windows before it escaped.

The riot was centred in the downtown area of Barrington and Hollis streets. Almost ten thousand sailors, soon joined by several thousand civilians, rampaged through the area—smashing, looting, and burning. Liquor stores were the initial targets. The one on Sackville Street was broken into first, followed by the main store on Hollis Street at midnight and the Buckingham Street store a half-hour later. Typically, a group of people—sailors and civilians—would smash the windows, get inside, and pass cases of booze to the waiting crowds outside. By 1:00 AM the looting was over, police stood guard at the liquor stores, and the shore patrol was busy rounding up all naval ratings and returning them to barracks.

The morning of May 8 dawned over a quiet city. Looters had long since dispersed and returned to barracks. The "disturbances" of the previous day were hardly mentioned in the morning papers. Despite the evidence of the destruction wrought by his men, Admiral Murray would not rescind his earlier orders giving them the day off. "If the civilians are to

*A large crowd gathers on Hollis Street during the Halifax V-E Day riots at about 4:00 PM on May 8, 1945.*

be allowed downtown to celebrate," he asked, "why not the navy?" Why not, indeed? The answer would soon be all too obvious.

At 1:00 PM on May 8, the wet canteen at *Stadacona* ran out of beer. After smashing beer bottles, about two thousand ratings spilled into Barrington Street and commandeered a streetcar. They ejected its operator and his passengers, broke its doors and seats, and took off towards the downtown. The streetcar was followed by a large mob. As they streamed southwards, they broke windows in the houses they passed. Larger plate-glass windows of the businesses they encountered were targeted as they reached the city centre, stores like T. Eaton Company, People's Credit Jewellers, Birks and Sons. The streets and sidewalks were soon covered in broken glass. As the mob moved on to Keith's Brewery, its camp followers stripped everything they could from broken shop-fronts.

Sometime between 1:30 and 4:30 the mob, worked into a considerable frenzy, charged the Sackville Street liquor store but was repulsed by a combination of civilian and military police. Mayor Butler relayed a request from the police chief to Admiral Murray for

HALIFAX V-E DAY CELEBRATION. HON. A.S. MAC MILLAN, PREMIER OF NOVA SCOTIA.

HALIFAX V-E DAY CELEBRATION. MUSIC BY P.L.F. BAND.

HALIFAX V-E DAY CELEBRATION. THOUSANDS GATHER FOR THE MORNING CELEBRATION ON THE GARRISON GROUNDS.

HALIFAX V-E DAY CELEBRATION. UNCLE MEL'S ARTISTS ENTERTAIN.

HALIFAX V-E DAY CELEBRATION. The TEEN AGERS CELEBRATE "KNUCKER HUCK"

VICTORY

LEADERS ANNOUNCE VICTORY

J. HAYWARD // BUCKINGHAM ST. HALIFAX                COPYRIGHT

*The official celebrations for V-E Day were held on the Garrison Grounds beside Citadel Hill, May 8, 1945. The varied programme included a speech by Premier A. S. MacMillan, music by the Princess Louise Fusiliers' band, and songs by Uncle Mel's Artists.*

additional help when it appeared police headquarters was about to be attacked. The admiral did not believe it, although he did send sixty-seven men from the shore patrol school to reinforce the police. Then he went off to a memorial service at the Garrison Grounds.

At Keith's Brewery, a mob of four thousand—mostly sailors—broke down the iron gate and stormed inside. When the owner, Colonel Sidney Oland, heard this, he went into the warehouse and joined his workers in passing each man a case of beer. Several members of the shore patrol, who had rushed there to stop the looting, helped Oland and his men give out the beer. When the booze was gone, the crowd left without causing substantial damage, although not before they let the still-hot, undrinkable beer in the pasteurizing plant run out into the gutter.

While this was going on, the three senior commanders of the navy, army, and air force were at the memorial service on the Garrison Grounds. At 3:00 PM, they were told of the liquor store looting. Murray immediately decided a tri-service parade through the city would calm down the rioters. The soldiers and airmen marched to the police station, while the sailors carried on to *Stadacona*. By the time they got there, nearly a third of the 375-man-strong naval contingent had slipped away to join their drunken comrades.

Only a few minutes before 6:00 PM, officials decided that the "celebrations" would end at 6:00, with a curfew to follow at 8:00 PM. The admiral and the mayor drove through the downtown in a sound truck, with Murray making most of the announcements: "This is Admiral Murray speaking. Go to your billets, your ships, your quarters, and your homes! This applies both to civilians and service personnel."

The rioting was largely over by midnight, except for drunken stragglers staggering back to barracks, and shore patrol and sailors pressed into service gathering up those who were passed out or too drunk to make it back on their own. Drunken sailors were thrown into trucks "like cordwood." The reckoning started the next day, when the police magistrate faced the biggest dock he had ever seen—211 rioters.

During two days of rioting, 6,987 cases of beer, 1,225 cases of wine, 2 cases of alcohol, and 55,392 quarts of spirits were looted from government liquor stores in Halifax, along with 30,516 quarts of beer from Keith's Brewery. The Liquor Commission subsequently recovered 1,140 quarts of spirits, 81 cases of beer, and 10 cases of wine. In Dartmouth, alcohol thefts totalled 5,256 quarts of beer, 1,692 quarts of wine, and 9,816 quarts of liquor, of which 550 bottles were recovered.

Property losses in Halifax were unofficially estimated at five million dollars and involved 564 firms, of which 207 were looted to some degree. Nearly 2,650 pieces of plate and other glass were broken, while a police car and a streetcar were set on fire and burned. Three people were killed and several hundred injured, mostly from broken glass.

As expected, the navy received the lion's share of blame for the riots. In a radio address to Haligonians shortly afterwards, Mayor Butler said, "I speak to the solemn protests of

*Civilians—including children—and sailors loot a small corner store during the Halifax V-E Day riots, May 8, 1945.*

the citizens against the Canadian Navy. It will be a long time before the people of Halifax forget this great crime." Admiral Murray offered the opinion that bootleggers were now "in possession of considerable stocks." He still believed in the innocence of most of his sailors however, and stated, "I am satisfied that, though service personnel were present during the whole afternoon, in almost all cases civilians led the assault and encouraged service personnel to take part."

## A ROYAL COMMISSION

SHORTLY AFTER THE RIOTS took place, the federal government ordered a Royal Commission into the incidents, headed by Supreme Court of Canada Justice Roy Kellock. On August 17, the results of the Commission were released. Kellock did not mince his words, placing responsibility for the riots on the navy's failure to control its service personnel. "Once started," his report read, "the development and continuance of the disorders were due to the failure of the naval command to put down the initial disorders on each of the two days."

With blinders firmly in place—typical of so many government reports—Kellock pointedly ignored other possible reasons for the disturbances and disputed any suggestion that the cause of the riots was resentment because of restaurants being closed. Incredibly, neither did he find any underlying bitterness on the part of service personnel against Halifax because of overcrowding and other discomforts. "The cause of the troubles of May 7 and 8 were, in my opinion, the same, namely the lack of planning to occupy the minds and the time of the ratings and keep them from wandering in large parties about the streets."

B. K. Sandwell, editor of the influential national weekly *Saturday Night* and writing under the pseudonym Lucy Van Gogh on May 25, shortly after the riots, formed his own opinion. He noted that servicemen had no great affection for Halifax, and there "was no reason why they should have." He was particularly damning in his assessment of the city. He stated that when war came and suddenly converted the city into one of the great ports of the world, it did not adjust to the changes thrust upon it.

"In fact," he went on, "it continues to be a small port town, with a way of life, and a set of by-laws, very much unlike those of the other great maritime municipalities." In particular, he condemned the restricted availability of alcohol, which could only be purchased

*A disabled streetcar sits empty on Barrington Street, while a shop owner boards up his window after the Halifax V-E Day riots.*

*Rear Admiral Leonard Murray inspects sailors at* HMCS Cornwallis *during the Second World War. It was during an inspection similar to this that Murray alienated almost the entire ship's company of* HMCS Algonquin *at the end of the war.*

from government liquor stores and taken home to be consumed, as totally impractical for service personnel living in barracks or aboard ships, where alcohol was not permitted. In most major port cities around the world, sailors and soldiers were provided with places where they could purchase alcoholic drinks and "consume them on the spot with their feet on a rail or their elbows on a table. But Halifax never got round to providing such places."

Federal Minister for the Naval Service Douglas Abbott expressed his regret for the riots, but also pointedly noted that "many of the naval ratings who took part in these unfortunate disturbances are the same men who have earned their country's gratitude for their courage and endurance in the long and arduous Atlantic campaign." Abbott also stated his support for Admiral Murray, of whom he said, "His responsibilities have been great, and upon his shoulders rested a heavy proportion of the burden of the Battle of the Atlantic...for however great may have been the rejoicing ashore, the U-boat had not at that time ceased."

The Royal Commission discovered that army and air personnel were controlled, kept in quarters, or provided with programmes. For the navy however, more than 9,000 sailors out of 13,306 in ships and shore establishments had left their units on May 7—in keeping with the navy's "open gangway" policy—and were ashore from 5:00 PM to 7:00 AM the next morning. The next day, 500 more went ashore. "It was not surprising," Kellock wrote, "that these large numbers of naval personnel went into the city. There was no adequate program to hold them away." Despite the findings of the Royal Commission, the rest of the country blamed Haligonians for the riots, mainly because of their treatment of sailors during the war.

In the end, Admiral Murray was held responsible for not exercising sufficient control over his sailors during the V-E Day riots. He resigned from the RCN on September 14, a resignation that was accepted with astonishing alacrity. Many people felt he was a scapegoat for the whole unfortunate affair, when his subordinates were the ones really at fault. His distinguished career ended without the recognition he fully deserved for his important role in the Battle of the Atlantic. Murray immediately moved to Britain, where he lived until his death in 1971.

"Yogi" Jensen was one naval officer who had little sympathy for Murray. After six hard years of war, much of it abroad, Jensen returned to Halifax in April 1945, by then a lieutenant, aboard HMCS *Algonquin*. When he arrived, he noted that Halifax was crowded with service personnel and "was quite a contrast to the places where we had been. It seemed to me that there was an unpleasant atmosphere about the city." *Algonquin*'s sailors got into trouble on their first night ashore, in contrast to every other port the ship had visited during the war.

Leave and de-ammunitioning of the ship were delayed a week until Murray "found it convenient to look us over." He inspected the ship's company "not saying a word to anyone, unsmiling, perhaps even hostile." When the admiral spoke to the crew, he said he was glad that he had only found one sailor wearing a suit made of diagonal serge, as it was against regulations. Then he "cautioned us against boastful behaviour and informed us that people on this side of the Atlantic had a role every bit as important as our own had been." He ended by warning that if anyone behaved inappropriately because of their experience, "he would be punished to the full extent."

Jensen was stunned. Not only was he completely unaware of what "diagonal serge" was, its relevance at the time was totally lost on him. Jensen called it "the most stupid speech to a ship's company that I have ever heard." He felt that "anyone in authority who had such an attitude was asking for trouble." It came as "no surprise" to him that on V-E Day a few weeks later, Halifax "suffered a riot and destruction by the navy and civilians such as no other city in the British Empire experienced."

*WRCNS personnel operate the switchboard at HMCS* Stadacona, *Halifax, March 3, 1943.*

CHAPTER 8

# SAILORS IN SKIRTS

### JENNY WREN

THE WOMEN'S ROYAL CANADIAN NAVAL SERVICE (WRCNS)—popularly
known as Wrens or Jenny Wrens—was formed in 1942 to fill a number of shore-
based jobs, which freed up men to serve at sea. In the spring of 1941, as the Second
World War approached the end of its second year, the demands for manpower to fill the
ranks of an expanding navy, army, and air force continued to grow. To help alleviate the
problem, National Defence Headquarters asked the three services what roles they thought
uniformed women might be able to perform. The navy, unlike the other two services, felt
all it would need was twenty women drivers and did not believe it would be necessary to

create a separate branch for females. It was an opinion that would soon change with the realities of the Battle of the Atlantic.

As the demand for men to crew ships rose during the next year, the navy decided to form a women's branch. In January 1942, the RCN signalled the British Admiralty for assistance in creating this new branch, with the urgent message, "Please send us a Mother Wren." In response, the RN sent three officers of the Women's Royal Naval Service to Canada to help establish the Canadian equivalent of their branch.

The RCN largely adopted the British model and the three British officers travelled across Canada promoting the new service. They were successful in attracting a number of applicants. Initially, candidates had to be white British subjects, between the ages of eighteen and forty-five, and without dependent children under the age of sixteen. Officer commissions could not be granted to anyone under twenty-one. These requirements changed over time. Exemptions were given for particularly suitable candidates up to forty-nine years of age. In 1943, the age requirement for cooks was raised to under fifty-six, while in 1944 racial restrictions were eliminated. Applicants also had to pass a medical examination and have attained a minimum of grade eight education, except for officers, who needed a university qualification or an equivalent.

## WOMEN'S WORK

DESPITE INTEGRATION INTO THE navy, women received less pay and benefits than their male counterparts, even when doing the same job. In the beginning, women were paid two-thirds of a man's basic rate, which was raised to four-fifths in July 1943. Senior military officers justified this differential on the grounds that men could be sent into combat, while women could not. Nevertheless, women in the service generally received better pay and benefits than their counterparts in civilian industry.

In May 1942, a memorandum sent to the Cabinet War Committee contained the following naval jobs and tasks that could be undertaken by females: administrative clerk, telephone switchboard operator, teleprinter operator, wireless telegraphic operator, cipher clerk, coder, cook, steward, messenger, elevator operator, and motor transport driver. As the war went on, additional jobs were added. In 1943, a newspaper advertisement listed the following new positions: wardroom attendant, quarters assistant, laundress, supply assistant, stenographer, confidential book corrector, postal clerk, secretary, pay writer, communications and operations specialist, sail maker, sick berth attendant, and regulator. By the end of the war, there were thirty-nine trades open to Wrens, compared to fifty-five for the Canadian Women's Army Corps and sixty-five for the RCAF Women's Division. More than 40 per cent of Wrens served in the Supply Branch.

Although many of these jobs were decidedly unglamorous, they were all important to the war effort, a fact recognized by Rear Admiral George Jones, the Vice Chief of the

*WRCNS coders at work in Halifax, June 1944.*

Naval Staff. While visiting a Wren school, he noted, "Many of these jobs are not spectacular, but they are vital to the service. They must be done—and done well—or the service will suffer."

## TRAINING THE WRENS

BY THE SUMMER OF 1942, there were two thousand applicants for the first course. Sixty-seven of them commenced a month-long officer training programme in Ottawa on August 29, while many of the remainder became leading Wrens. In mid-September, twenty-eight of these women appeared before the first Wrens officer selection board and twenty-two were appointed as officers in the RCN, the first women in any of His Majesty's navies anywhere in the Commonwealth to carry the King's commission. Upon graduation on October 1, the Wrens' first officers were either sent to the Grandview School for Girls, a requisitioned rehabilitation and correctional facility in Galt (now Cambridge), Ontario, to set up the Wrens' basic training centre or became recruiting officers across the country.

The WRCNS training centres at Galt and elsewhere were known as stone frigates in naval terminology and commissioned as HMC Ships. The training centre at Galt was

HMCS *Conestoga*. It conducted a three-week basic training course centred on making a rapid transition from civilian to naval life for Probationary Wrens. New Wrens were paid ninety cents a day while undergoing training, which increased to ninety-five cents on graduation. Physical training, drill, and naval traditions and customs formed a large part of the curriculum. Once the Wrens graduated from the basic course, they were sent to their new jobs or on to further training in Toronto, St. Hyacinthe, or Halifax.

Like their male counterparts, the women had to learn new terminology for most of their physical surroundings as well as several objects, keeping up the long-standing naval tradition that no matter where sailors were, they longed to be at sea and gave familiar items around them naval names. Fiddy Greer, a wartime Wren who wrote about her experiences in her book titled *The Girls of the King's Navy*, recounted an occasion during her training in Ontario before she got to Halifax, when one Wren took this tradition a little too far. Greer and her mates were quartered in the Preston Springs Hotel, which was suitably rechristened *Jellicoe* after a famous British admiral.

Their training days at *Jellicoe* were long and busy, so when the girls climbed into their bunks at 10:30 PM for lights out, they all quickly fell into a deep sleep. One night at around one o'clock in the morning, they were startled from their slumber by a loud whistle and someone shouting, "Abandon Ship! Abandon Ship!" It took the sleepy Wrens some time to realize that in fact a fire drill was in progress. If the Duty Watch Wren had simply yelled "Fire! Fire!" it would have elicited a far speedier response. After "mustering on deck for

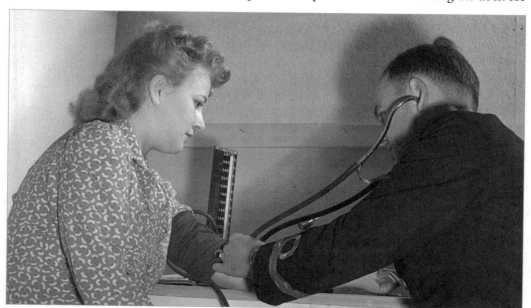

*Rosamund Fiddes is medically examined by Surgeon Lieutenant T. E. Wilson at the Joint Service Headquarters, Vancouver, May 14, 1943.*

roll call" (gathering on the lawn), it was discovered that one Wren was missing. After a second confirmatory count, she was found safe and sound snuggled in her bunk, obviously preferring "to go down with the ship." "However," Greer noted, "the ship remained afloat, and she could be seen swabbing the decks each evening for quite some time afterwards."

## WRENS IN HALIFAX

IN HALIFAX, THE TRAINING CENTRE was HMCS *Cornwallis*, which was initially established in *Stadacona*. Accommodation was a problem, and new Wrens crowded into the Wren Block, originally built for signallers on course, as well as a temporary annex hastily constructed beside it. Many of the girls were unenthusiastic about the living arrangements. In *Great Coats and Glamour Boots*, author Carolyn Gossage recorded some of their impressions. According to one former Wren, "In Halifax it was unbelievable. You got a clean sheet every two months."

Food arrangements were not much better. Another Wren described how the girls got their meals when they were on the midnight shift. They would enter the dining room, pitch black because all the cooks were out back in the kitchen. Pre-cut bread was laid out on the counter, covered with a clean white cloth. While one of the Wrens flipped the light switch on, the others would whip off the cloths "and the bread would be crawling with cockroaches," which "just vanished—as if into thin air." After that, "Nobody was very anxious to help themselves to bread."

Fiddy Greer also had occasion to deal with nocturnal insects in Halifax. After several weeks of examining bites on their bodies each morning, she and her cabin mates came to the unanimous conclusion that they had bedbugs. On reporting this to the Wren medical officer (MO), they were informed that bites alone could not be considered as conclusive evidence; they would have to produce a body—dead or alive.

Since bedbugs burrow deep into blankets and mattresses during the day and only come out to feed on their human hosts during the night, the Wrens came up with a strategy to capture one in a plan of attack worthy of their new occupations. Thirty minutes after lights out (to give the creatures time to come out of their hiding places), every occupant in Greer's cabin "leaped out of her bunk, threw back her blankets, and with a flashlight spotlighting her bed, frantically searched for the required body."

In a few seconds, "there was a shout of victory (mingled with horror) from Jeannie, who was probably the most fastidious girl in the entire [WRCNS]." In the middle of her bed she had discovered one of the "loathsome" creatures. "Her enthusiasm overcame her caution, and she pounced upon it with such vigour that it was barely distinguishable from a mashed currant." The girls carefully collected the bug's squashed remains, placed them in a matchbox lined with cotton batten, and the next morning "ceremoniously presented our corpus delecti to the Medical Officer." The operation worked. The next weekend the Wren Block was fumigated, which entailed a much-welcomed forty-eight-hour pass for all Wrens.

Life within the confines of the Wren Block was not all bad, although Greer imagined it was similar to living within the "cloistered wall of a convent." She felt the Wrens accommodated in the five-storey building could have lived quite comfortably without ever having to go outside. Besides their cabins, there was a sick bay, post office, beauty salon, canteen (dry only—no alcohol), mess, galley, tailor shop, laundry rooms (no washing machines—only cement tubs), and the fo'c'sle. Located on the top floor, the fo'c'sle was the place for Wrens to relax, write letters, listen to the radio, smoke, catch up on gossip, and knit sweaters and socks.

A constant fear among the Wrens' superior officers was that some of their girls would get pregnant, necessitating an automatic and quick release from the service. This concern about Wrens' sexuality led to attempts to control it. According to Greer, one of the methods used for keeping their sex lives under surveillance was not realized by the Wrens for some time. Each month they attended what they quaintly referred to as "Blue Box Day Parade," when they lined up and signed for a box of sanitary napkins.

It never occurred to them that, while they had to provide their own personal care items such as soap, deodorant, and toothpaste, the navy gave them this item as a free issue.

*Members of the WRCNS strike an "informal" pose in their Halifax dormitory, May 1943.*

When one girl was called before the Wren MO and asked if she had any problems she wished to discuss, she said she did not have any. Why then, the MO wondered, had she not attended a Blue Box Day Parade for the last three months? The Wren stated that she preferred a new development called a tampon and simply never bothered to collect her blue boxes. The story quickly made the rounds of the entire Wren population in Halifax, and from that day forward none of them ever missed another Blue Box Day Parade.

About a thousand Wrens served in Halifax, and life for them was even more restrictive than for male sailors. Their curfew was very early—normally 10:00 PM—with one midnight pass a week. Midnight passes were necessary to go to a movie, which required two hours waiting in line before getting in. The city's few downtown restaurants also had long lines of people waiting to get in, especially the most popular, the Green Lantern, known to service personnel as the "Green Latrine." As well, Wrens were not allowed in the wet canteen at *Stadacona*, for a long time the only place in the city where a sailor could buy a beer and sit and enjoy it.

## UNIFORMS

THE RCN'S FIRST ATTEMPT at a women's uniform was described by one Wren as "really dowdy—made of heavy blue serge with a pork pie hat. No self-respecting woman would join up to wear something like that." After experiments with various styles of dress, by July 1943 the Wren uniform was navy blue in winter and light blue in summer, with a white shirt, black tie, black stockings, and black shoes. The pork pie hat was finally replaced with a tricorn or the standard sailor's "roundrig," depending on rank. Wrens also carried a "pochette," a small purse that was considered a part of the uniform. In wintertime, two additional items of clothing protected the Wrens from the weather, known affectionately as "glamour boots" and "passion pants." Officers, like their RN counterparts, wore blue lace stripes and a diamond on their sleeves, instead of the gold lace and executive curl worn by males. Their uniform became a major point of pride for all Wrens and was the deciding factor that caused many to join. According to Greer, wearing a uniform seemed to change the women who wore them. "We were transformed into a sameness that affected strong feelings of camaraderie and unity. We were Wrens...and we were very proud of it."

The uniform was not the only reason women joined, of course. Some were motivated by having a relative, a friend, or even a boyfriend in the navy. One Wren told Gossage that a lot of the women with whom she served had lost someone dear to them in action. She recalled two in particular, "who would normally have nothing in common if they'd been civilians—but they became fast friends because of this common bond of having been widowed." Some joined for the excitement of being part of the great adventure that was the war and the chance to see other parts of Canada or even overseas. Others felt that, as the last women's branch of the service to be formed, there might be less competition and

*Wrens model the types of uniforms worn in 1942: (L–R) Officers' winter uniform, officers' summer uniform, ratings' winter uniform, and ratings summer uniform.*

greater career opportunities. But most were motivated by the simple desire to help their country and contribute to the war effort.

Almost all Wrens quickly discovered an important and attractive feature of military and naval life that men had known for centuries: the camaraderie shared by those in uniform working and living together, rising above self to contribute to a common cause. "We came in as individuals concerned with our own well-being," Wren Doris Cale explained in Lisa Banister's *Equal to the Challenge: An Anthology of Women's Experiences During World War II*, "but we soon became a community working towards a common goal of supporting the navy's war effort." When she was later promoted and entitled to a private living space, Cale said she missed living with the girls to whom she had grown so close.

## WAR WORK

ANOTHER CONTRIBUTOR TO *Equal to the Challenge*, Janet Watt was among the first draft of Wrens sent to Halifax, where she trained as a postal clerk. She ended up working for a lieutenant whom she had known back in Montreal—where they both were employed

*WRCNS personnel sort mail at the Fleet Mail Office, Halifax, March 3, 1943: (L–R) Wrens F. A. Padgett, R. K. Dwyer, and M. S. Macdonald.*

by the T. Eaton Company. When she was discharged after the end of the war as a leading Wren, a captain noted that she had been recommended for officer training three times. "Why didn't you accept?" he inquired. She replied that all her friends were leading Wrens. "I didn't want to leave them," she said, and "preferred to stay with my friends."

Although Watt felt it sounded horrible, she recalled that she "actually had a very good time during the war. I enjoyed my work, and did it with pride." She believed that serving in the navy taught her "discipline and people skills." She was glad for the experience and "wouldn't have missed it." Although Halifax was not really that far from Montreal, it did "broaden my horizons in so many ways."

In the joint RCN/RCAF plot room at Halifax, one of Gossage's Wren correspondents noted, "We kept track of all shipping on the North Atlantic. Gales, broken ships, U-boats, and changes of course were part of our daily life," making the war seem "very close." Another Wren agreed: "Most Canadians had no idea just how close those German U-boats got— way up the St. Lawrence." Occasionally, the Halifax plotter Wrens "would stay up half the night, after their shifts, because of all the action on the board," as they wanted to see what happened. The plotters were "extremely bright" and "devoted to their jobs." The constantly changing operational plot meant that many of them put in long overtime hours, but they "contributed a great deal" to the war effort. Another Wren stationed in Halifax echoed these feelings of being close to the action at sea. She recalled that while attending church,

*Wrens assisted navy and air force duty officers in joint RCN/RCAF plot rooms in Halifax and St. John's (pictured) keep track of all ships in the North Atlantic.*

the minister would often announce during the sermon that ships were being sunk right outside the harbour. "You'd hear the sirens and the ambulance," she noted, from emergency personnel responding to the tragedy.

Carol Hendry from Toronto joined the WRCNS in March 1943. After basic training at Galt, she was slated for "operations," and went to Ottawa for officer training, by then extended to five weeks. On graduation as a sub-lieutenant, Hendry was posted to Halifax, to what she termed "a wonderful new project called 'The Tactical Table.'" The aim of the table was to teach escort vessel commanders and their key officers what to expect in taking a convoy from Halifax to Britain.

According to Hendry, "There was what you called a 'Tactical Game' given to about six escort vessels." Representatives from the escort vessels were around the tactical table, but could not see what the controllers were doing, just as if they were on their own ship. The controllers would present a problem—such as submarines in the vicinity—to the escort ships' officers, who would state what they would do in the circumstances. Hendry and her colleagues would pass sightings or bearings to various objects to the officers, who would then send back their instructions, which the controllers in turn would plot on the table. The game proceeded for an hour or so, when "the senior officer would tell what they had done right and what they had done wrong, and what they should have done." Hendry described it as "a wonderful lesson."

TOP *Wrens Margaret Horn, Shirley Shoebottom, and Camilla Balcombe assist Lieutenant E. G. Aust at the tactical table, Halifax, June 1944.*

BOTTOM *WRCNS Writer M. McDonald working in the navigation library at HMCS Kings, Halifax, March 3, 1943.*

*Wren Gibbs delivers a message to the officers of the minesweeper* HMCS Esquimalt *at Halifax, February 2, 1943.*

After a year on the tactical table, Hendry became a training staff officer under the training commander in August 1944. In that job, she was responsible for helping to set up training for the crews of all the ships that came into Halifax. Other Wrens worked in several other jobs in the busy port. For those employed as sick berth attendants in the RCN hospital, the task they dreaded most was giving needles to male patients in their posteriors. The sailors took great delight in embarrassing the young girls. Some Wrens had unique jobs. Three of them worked on the spotting table in the gunnery training centre, becoming the only gunnery Wrens in the entire country, while three more worked in the headquarters for the navy's fleet of anti-submarine motor launches. Another six Wrens were drummers in the *Stadacona* band.

As a writer/typist, Fiddy Greer was assigned to Pay Division 11 in Halifax. Although most of the navy's shore operations had been moved from the dockyard into *Stadacona* in July 1943, Pay Division 11 stayed in the dockyard, close to Jetty Five and the ships that tied up there. The pay ledgers that Greer maintained contained the crews of a few minesweepers and frigates, but most were from the workhorse corvettes that provided the bulk of convoy escorts.

Like Greer, Doris Cale was a pay writer, only she worked in Pay Division IV in the administration building, where she "had a magnificent view of Halifax harbour." From it,

*WRCNS personnel embark on a troopship at Halifax destined for Britain, February 1944.*

she "could see the convoys going out to sea on their way to Britain, with their decks laden with supplies and even vehicles." Besides paying the crews of RCN ships, Cale's office also paid the naval ratings on the Defensively Equipped Merchant Ships, known as DEMS. Many of these sailors lost their lives when their vessels were sunk, and the pay writers had to close their accounts. "That was a sad task," Cale reflected.

While the army and air force posted females to Britain in August 1942, the first Wrens to go abroad went to Washington in April 1943 to work for the Canadian Joint Staff. One-sixth of all Wrens served outside of Canada—about 50 in either Washington or New York, 503 in Britain, and 586 in Newfoundland, which was considered overseas at the time as it was not yet a part of Canada. Of all the locations where Wrens served—at home and abroad—those assigned to the East Coast, especially to Halifax, came closest to the harsh reality of colossal battle waged in the North Atlantic.

## REDUCED, REACTIVATED, INTEGRATED

WOMEN FROM ALL WALKS of life joined the WRCNS during the Second World War. Once recruiting began, it continued until February 1945, having attracted more than sixty-five hundred women. Despite several arguments for the continuation of women in the service, the WRCNS was disbanded and the last women were released in December 1946.

After the Korean War started in 1950, the RCN began to enrol women in 1951, this time into the Women's Reserve of the RCNR. Sixty officers and 650 ratings completed their initial training at HMCS *Cornwallis* in the Annapolis Valley. In January 1955, the cabinet approved a women's regular force component for the RCN, which came into being in 1956 under Commander Isabel MacNeill, a wartime senior WRCNS officer from Halifax. These women were still called Wrens, but they were full-fledged members of the RCN—their officers even wore gold braid.

In 1961, a committee was established to study the whole question of Wrens in the personnel structure of the navy. It made a number of recommendations, which the Naval Board—the RCN's highest authority—accepted. This was followed in 1964 by the Landymore Report on the RCN's critical personnel shortages, which recommended the restriction of women to positions in which "men cannot be suitably or effectively employed and where civilians possessed of the required skills were not obtainable." It also proposed employing them temporarily in under-strength trades, but only until enough men were available. By 1965, there were only 288 Wrens in the RCN.

*WRCNS radar plotters D. C. Morrison, V. R. Ward, and P. M. Fotheringham participate in air station familiarization for the Maritime Warfare School at HMCS Shearwater, November 3, 1955, as they prepare to fly in a Sikorsky HO4S "Horse" helicopter.*

Although Wrens were still not allowed to go to sea, women filled many important support jobs ashore, especially in administration, food services, and finance. One of their jobs was working in the naval station at Shelburne, Nova Scotia, which monitored part of the chain of underwater listening posts in the Atlantic Ocean, known as Sound Surveillance Under the Sea (sosus). sosus could detect snorkelling or surfaced submarines at very long distances and occasionally even identify them. Once detected, maritime patrol aircraft would follow up contacts and ships might be dispatched as well. It was perhaps the most important operational duty the Wrens had during the Cold War.

*The destroyer* HMCS Nootka *fires at an enemy truck convoy during the night of June 1, 1952, somewhere off the east coast of North Korea.*

CHAPTER 9

# CONFLICT IN THE LAND OF THE MORNING CALM

INVASION

A T FOUR O'CLOCK ON THE MORNING of Sunday, June 25, 1950, the peace and quiet of the Land of the Morning Calm—as Korea had traditionally been known for centuries—was shattered by one hundred thousand soldiers of the Democratic People's Republic of Korea as they swarmed across the border and attacked the small and ill-equipped army of the Republic of Korea. The all-out invasion against the south had been launched in an attempt to forcibly reunify the peninsula, separated since the end of the Second World War.

Hostilities between North Korea and South Korea eventually drew supporters of both nations into a fight which raged back and forth along the length and breadth of the Korean

Peninsula, in the air above it, and on the seas surrounding it. North Korea was openly supported by Communist China and somewhat less so by the Soviet Union, against South Korea and the United Nations (UN). Some sixteen nations contributed combat forces to the UN operation, led by the United States, with only the American and the British contributions exceeding the Canadian one. It was a strange place to fight a war. In the opinion of American Secretary of State Dean Atchison, "If the best minds in the world set out to find us the worst possible location in the world to fight this damnable war, politically and militarily, the unanimous choice would have been Korea!"

The tiny gunboat navy of North Korea had been neutralized early on (there was only one action at sea during the entire war, on July 1, 1950), giving the naval forces of the nine countries that contributed warships to the UN operation virtually complete freedom of movement in the waters that bordered the Korean Peninsula on three sides. With no enemy navy to fight, ships of the participating UN navies were limited to certain tasks: blockading the enemy coast, escorting aircraft carriers, coastal bombarding of shore batteries and trains (the latter a skill at which the RCN became particularly adept), searching sampans and junks, destroying mines, evacuating soldiers and civilians trapped in bridgeheads, and bringing humanitarian aid to isolated South Korean fishing villages.

## CANADA ANSWERS THE CALL

ALMOST UNKNOWN, AND OVERSHADOWED by the large part the Canadian Army played, was the navy's involvement in the Korean War, including four ships from Halifax. On July 5, 1950, just eleven days after the North invaded the South, three RCN warships departed Esquimalt—the first Canadian contribution to the war. The readiness of the RCN was remarked upon in the House of Commons, where the Minister of National Defence described the navy as "nearer to being on active service than any of our other services." Flying the UN flag at their foremasthead, the three ships of Canada's Pacific Destroyer Division sailed into the large, bustling harbour at Sasebo, Japan, on July 30, under leaden skies. The port was used by UN vessels and was about 160 kilometres from the territorial waters of Korea.

Eventually, while HMC Ships *Cayuga*, *Athabaskan*, *Sioux*, and *Crusader* from Esquimalt took part in the early stages of the war, HMC Ships *Nootka*, *Huron*, *Iroquois*, and *Haida* from Halifax participated later, relieving their western counterparts. Except for *Crusader*, a former RN C class destroyer, and *Sioux*, an RN V class one, the RCN ships were Tribals. At any one time, the RCN kept three operational destroyers on station—a task that stretched the already slim resources of the navy to the limit. On August 15, *Cayuga* fired the first of 130,000 rounds lobbed by Canadian warships during hundreds of bombardments against the enemy over the next three years. It was the first time since 1945 that any RCN ship had fired her guns in combat.

*HMCS* Nootka *astern the aircraft carrier USS* Bataan *between Midway Island and Japan, February 1952.*

## *NOOTKA* BATTLES BRIDGES

IN EARLY 1951, the first ships from Halifax arrived in Korean waters. *Nootka* sailed into Sasebo in mid-January 1951, replacing *Sioux*, while *Huron* relieved *Cayuga* later in mid-March. Even though the North Korean navy had been eliminated as a threat, there remained other dangers to UN ships. Enemy mines had been laid in many coastal areas and gunfire from numerous shore batteries posed an ever-present threat.

On January 25, 1951, Canadian destroyers came under enemy fire for the first time, after *Cayuga* and *Nootka* had finished their part in a UN bombardment of the port of

*HMCS* Nootka *fires her 40-mm Bofors guns, June 1952.*

Inchon. In *Korea: Canada's Forgotten War* by John Melady, Lorne Barton, a stoker from the Halifax-based *Nootka*, recalled what happened next: "Then, just as we were leaving the place, somebody started shooting at us. The Old Man ordered us to swing around and we moved in closer and opened up on them." None of the enemy's rounds hit the Canadian ships. The North Koreans were not so lucky; the 4-inch guns of the two RCN warships quickly silenced the shore batteries with devastatingly accurate fire. Then, for good measure, *Nootka* closed to within range of her 40-mm Bofors guns and sprayed the area before departing.

Although RCN ships had operated primarily on the west coast of the peninsula, in late May *Nootka* moved to the east coast and participated in shelling the railway line and roads that ran close to the shore. The sea conditions were better there, allowing the ships to get much closer inshore than on the other side of Korea. The first target assigned to *Nootka*'s captain, the flamboyant Commander Fraser Fraser-Harris of Halifax, was a bridge spanning a gully between two tunnels near Songjin. Fraser-Harris believed that explosives would do the job better than gunfire, so he dispatched a nineteen-man armed landing party, including a five-man demolition crew, to carry out the task in a motor cutter. Just then, fog moved in, rendering any gunfire support from *Nootka* ineffective. On the other hand, the fog provided much-needed cover for the cutter.

As the cutter approached the shore, the only noise was the steady chug-chug of its motor, followed by the soft sound of it grounding on the sandy beach. Suddenly, about half a dozen North Korean soldiers appeared out of the rocky cliffs behind the beach and began firing at the sailors. The Canadians immediately returned fire and, in accordance with their orders, made a hasty withdrawal. In future, Fraser-Harris relied on *Nootka*'s guns to do the job. He did not have long to wait.

*Nootka*'s next objective was a particularly difficult target, a bridge that had magically resisted all previous attempts to destroy it. Every time UN ships succeeded in damaging it, Korean workers repaired it during the night. The sailors nicknamed it the "Rubber Bridge." Fraser-Harris decided a close-in mission was necessary—despite the potential threat from enemy mines near the shore—which he christened Operation Squeegee. In the absence of any minesweepers in the area, the crew came up with a short-term but effective substitute.

Towing a wire between them, two motor cutters swept a channel ahead of *Nootka*, while the ship used her sonar to search for mines. Just to be safe, she also fired a pattern of 300-pound Squid mortar bombs ahead of her, which were intended to be used against submarines but could certainly detonate a mine. *Nootka* got twelve hundred metres offshore without encountering any mines. As had happened to the lone cutter at the previous bridge, soldiers suddenly appeared from the tunnels. The crew responded instantly, firing their 4-inch guns. Because of the short range, the 40-mm Bofors guns were able to add their fire. With the enemy soldiers killed or driven back, the Halifax sailors turned their

*HMCS Nootka fires a Squid mortar in the Yellow Sea, March 1952.*

attention to the train trestle and, joined by the USS *Stickell*'s 5-inch guns, fired at will. True to its name, the bridge refused to fall but was so badly damaged it could no longer be used. A cutter-load of fresh fish, killed by the Squid mortar, crowned the day's operations.

## TRAINBUSTER'S CLUB

A POPULAR FORM OF HARASSMENT developed against the North Koreans. "Trainbusting" was the shelling by naval ships of trains that were running on the coastal railway. Entry to the exclusive Trainbuster's Club was limited to any ship that destroyed a train's engine by bombardment. When a USN vessel blew up two trains in one day, according to the navy's official history of the Korean War, the RCN "entered into the spirit of this game with the greatest of enthusiasm, and before the end of hostilities had destroyed proportionally far and away more trains than had the ships of any other nation."

Members of the club destroyed a total of twenty-eight trains, with the RCN accounting for eight. West Coast ships wrecked six of these. *Crusader*, which became the undisputed champion of all the navies, had four kills. *Haida*, the last of the eight RCN destroyers to appear in theatre, destroyed at least eight rail cars shortly after she arrived from Halifax. She then accounted for the remaining two kills, both on her last patrol in May 1953.

*The destroyer* HMCS Haida *departs Halifax, bound for Korea, September 27, 1952.*

## R & R

SAILORS WERE ENTITLED TO R & R (Rest and Recreation) leave during a tour of duty in Korea. Normally very little rest was involved, and R & R became known as I & I (Intoxication and Intercourse). Sasebo, the temporary home port for dozens of UN ships and thousands of sailors, was not a good leave port. There were no night spots, only one good dining establishment, and no large department stores. But there were brothels. Ed Meyer, who served on *Cayuga* during the war and later chronicled the RCN's experience in *Thunder in the Morning Calm*, noted, "there were brothels on every street. ('Hey, Canada boy-san! I take you to heaven, ni?')." Some were large, others were one-woman operations.

Although all brothels were licensed, most had no medical supervision. Perhaps as many as 98 per cent of prostitutes were infected with venereal disease. This soon translated into a high incidence of VD—variously known as the Great Green Bubble, Cupid's Measles, Aphrodite's Revenge, and Sasebo Flu in the colourful language of the lower deck. Sailors who contracted VD were immediately disallowed their rum issue, denied leave for a minimum of thirty days, and had to report to sick bay every day for treatment. In addition,

*If R & R was not available, there was always homemade entertainment aboard ship. Officers of HMCS Nootka host their South Korean allies at a movie night, August 1952, off the Korean coast. The ship's captain, Commander Richard Steele, is seated on the right.*

they could only use a certain roped-off section of the heads, nicknamed Chancre Alley or the Rose Room.

Tokyo was a favourite haunt, and for many a prairie farm boy or Maritime down-homer, five days—which also meant five nights—in the bright lights of the city's famed entertainment district—the Ginza—was an otherworldly experience. In the time-honoured tradition of sailors let loose in any port around the world, most of the men were looking for two things: women and booze. In post-Second World War Japan, there were plenty of both available at unbelievably cheap prices.

In *Deadlock in Korea*, author Ted Barris recounts the experiences of a couple of sailors from *Huron*, who visited the hotels and bathhouses where female "cultural guides" were available for "cultural experiences." According to Leading Seaman Glenn Wilberforce, "We called them pompom houses. They weren't like normal brothels. They were clean and respectable." John Rigo, a stoker in *Huron*, noted that once a sailor picked out a woman he liked and paid the "mama-san," "Then you had that girl for the night." The sailor would go into the girl's room and put on a kimono, and then perhaps dance a bit. "If you felt amorous, you'd go into the room and then come out and dance some more." The girl was the sailor's for the whole night for five hundred yen—about two dollars.

In Hong Kong, another favourite R & R destination, Canadian sailors were confronted by seagoing "pompom girls." Moored to buoys in the stream, RCN ships would be approached by sampans bearing prostitutes and their madam, who would loudly call out the services her girls offered. Meyer noted they claimed that "good, old-fashioned 'pompom' was beneficial for all, as it reduced the tensions which had built up over weeks at sea." Invariably turned away by the officer of the day, the madams would depart, shaking their heads "in disbelief that anyone would refuse the convenience of a house call."

## *IROQUOIS* VERSUS SHORE BATTERIES

HMCS *IROQUOIS*, THE FIFTH OF SIX Tribal class destroyers to serve during the war, arrived in Sasebo on June 12, 1952, six weeks after leaving Halifax, and sailed for Korean waters eleven days later. Her sailors were struck by the destitution of the Koreans. After one occasion when Canadian ships helped evacuate some South Koreans, Denton Wessels, an eighteen-year-old crewman in *Iroquois*, told Melady, "I had never seen poverty until I saw Korea....I learned a lot from [the war]. I learned how good we have things in this country." His shipmate Jim Chapman echoed the sentiment. While sailors were lost at sea due to accidents or rough seas, the first of *Iroquois*'s three tours in Korean waters was to be a particularly poignant one, resulting in the only RCN combat deaths of the entire war.

Thirty-six-year-old Commander Bill Landymore was *Iroquois*'s captain. Landymore was originally from Brantford, Ontario, and had joined the RCN in 1936, seeing action during the Second World War in the Arctic, Atlantic, and Pacific oceans. As a lieutenant in the destroyer HMCS *Fraser* in June 1940, he survived a collision with a British cruiser

*The destroyer* HMCS Iroquois *pulls away from dockside in Halifax on her way to her first tour of duty in Korea, April 21, 1952.*

that cut *Fraser* in two off the coast of France. Five months later, he was serving in HMCS *Margaree*, *Fraser*'s replacement, when her bow was sliced off in a collision with a merchantman in a westbound Atlantic convoy.

Landymore developed a close rapport with his crew; under him, *Iroquois* was perhaps the happiest RCN ship of the eight that served in Korean waters. On September 27, three and a half months after arriving in Korea, Landymore and *Iroquois* sailed for a new mission off the east coast of the peninsula. Landymore was in charge of a task unit of five USN destroyers and two South Korean torpedo boats, and spent the next few days patrolling the area. It was a dangerous sector, so the lookouts were paying sharp attention, and the gun crews were closed up at all times. The ship had already been shelled once. Fortunately, the rounds fell short.

The next day, as *Iroquois* steamed slowly along the rugged coast leading the American destroyers, an eagle-eyed lookout on one of the ships spotted a large-calibre gun emplacement in a cave halfway up a hillside, which commanded the strait through which the convoy was sailing. Landymore ordered the Americans to use their main armament against the gun, but all missed in spite of firing several rounds. He then moved the ships in closer and called for another salvo, which again missed.

Telling the other ships to hold their fire, Landymore took *Iroquois* in as close as he dared, telling his gunnery officer to "display to the Americans the fine art of naval gunnery." Taking extra care in the laying and training of the guns, the gunnery officer gave the order to fire. Instantly from the mouth of the cave a single explosion erupted, at once destroying the gun, its crew, and ammunition. The navy's honour had been satisfied.

## DEADLY INCIDENT

UNDER CLEAR SKIES ON OCTOBER 2, just about a week after her first engagement, *Iroquois* was again on patrol when she responded to a call for assistance from the American destroyer USS *Marsh*, which had come under fire from shore batteries. When he arrived on the scene, Landymore ordered the United States ship to provide backup as he took his vessel close to shore. For two and a half hours, *Iroquois* fired round after round into the mouth of a train tunnel undergoing repairs and at two shore batteries, which remained silent. With her firing complete, the ship turned seaward to leave the area, momentarily beam on to the enemy.

The shore batteries opened fire immediately and their third shell hit the ship directly below the bridge, just aft of the "B" gun turret. The force of the impact blew members of the gun crew off their feet, knocking some unconscious and putting others into various states of shock. As choking, acrid smoke enveloped the area, several things happened at once. By sheer willpower, lightly wounded members of the gun crew struggled back to their positions and soon got "B" gun back in action, adding its fire to that already pouring forth from "A" gun. Without firing a shot in support, the USS *Marsh* turned and fled, an action that *Iroquois*'s sailors never forgave.

On the bridge, Commander Landymore ordered the engine room to lay heavy smoke to cover the destroyer's dash out of range of the shore batteries at full speed, as a medical party made its way to "B" gun deck. The sight that greeted them was quite horrific. There was a gaping hole in the ship just aft of the gun housing, and beside it lay the bodies of an officer and a sailor, both of whom had taken the full blast of the explosion and been killed instantly. Nearby lay the bodies of three other seamen, all severely wounded. Eight others, including three Nova Scotians, suffered light wounds from blast and flying fragments.

Each of the wounded was quickly examined in turn by the ship's doctor, and then moved aft and bedded down. For several hours, the doctor devoted all of his attention to the critically injured sailors as Landymore raced towards a Danish hospital ship, lying at anchor several kilometres south. As *Iroquois* sped southward, her captain, his voice breaking, announced over the ship's PA system that the most severely wounded sailor had died and there was no longer any reason to proceed to the hospital ship. The next day, the two remaining seriously wounded sailors were transferred to an American tanker on its way to Japan, along with the bodies of the three dead men, the RCN's only combat deaths of the entire war. They were subsequently buried in the Commonwealth War Cemetery near Yokohama, Japan.

## "RELENTLESS IN CHASE"

LANDYMORE THEN ADDRESSED his crew again, reminding them of *Iroquois*'s proud record from the Second World War and of the ship's motto, "Relentless in Chase." He told them how the motto originated with the tribe for which the ship had been named and how Iroquois warriors, once they defeated an enemy, would "run them to the ground so that none would escape." And that, he promised them, was how they would treat the batteries that had caused *Iroquois*'s casualties. Two hours later, *Iroquois* steamed into the waters where the damage had been inflicted upon her the day before. This time she was alone.

The ship's badge of HMCS Iroquois displayed a stern Iroquois warrior.

*Iroquois* raced in with all guns blazing, as a single spotter plane circled overhead to report the fall of shot. The North Korean guns opened up immediately in response, but the ship had the advantage as a moving target and the shore batteries were unable to hit her. In short order, the Canadian gunners put the main batteries out of action, and then, aided by reports from the airborne observer, began to systematically annihilate the smaller batteries. Shell after shell slammed home from *Iroquois*, until the spotter radioed that he could see no further targets. He then added, in almost awed tones, that in his long service career he "had never seen as fine a display of pinpoint shooting." Once again, *Iroquois* had satisfied Canadian naval honour and more than lived up to her motto. Landymore was awarded the Order of the British Empire and a Mention-in-Dispatches for his service in Korea.

## *HURON*'S HUMILIATION

*HURON*'S FIRST TOUR IN 1951 was uneventful and filled with the usual tasks of carrier screening, mine removal, and searching small boats, although she did damage a train. Her second tour in 1953 was a particularly unfortunate experience. On July 7, she was assigned to a patrol protecting the island of Yang-do, just off the northeast coast of North Korea.

The patrol area included a narrow strait between the island and the mainland, less than eight hundred metres wide, which was often fog-bound.

On July 12, a daytime southbound transit of the strait was achieved in the fog without incident, but at midnight, just as the watch changed, *Huron* came about to commence her northbound run. The fog was thicker, reducing visibility, and navigation was complicated by wave action. Running blind, with only her radar to guide her and her captain, Commander Richard Chenoweth, in his cabin, the two officers left in charge accidentally ran *Huron* aground on the island's rocky shoals just after midnight.

Fearing the worst, a party was dispatched over the side to inspect the damage. It was bad. The shoals had pushed in the front twenty-seven metres of the ship's thin hull and her sonar dome, which protruded from the bottom of the ship, was jammed into the rocks. When dawn came and the fog lifted, *Huron* would be a sitting duck, within the range of eight Korean shore batteries. Desperation drove the crew into action as they did everything they could to lighten her bows. Anything that was not permanently attached was either moved aft—ammunition, anchors, anchor chains, storage lockers, compartments, freezers—or thrown overboard, even the ship's piano.

Other UN ships soon learned of *Huron*'s predicament and rushed to the scene to lend whatever support they could, including the battleship USS *Missouri*—the famed "Mighty Mo" of the Second World War. Through superhuman efforts and with the assistance of a tug, by mid-morning the crew had worked *Huron* off the island. The damage was so extensive, however, that any forward movement put too much pressure on the weakened bow and threatened to open it up. Chenoweth had to steam backwards all the way to Sasebo, six hundred kilometres away, at a speed of three knots. The trip took over a week, until July 20.

*The destroyer* HMCS Huron *at sea.*

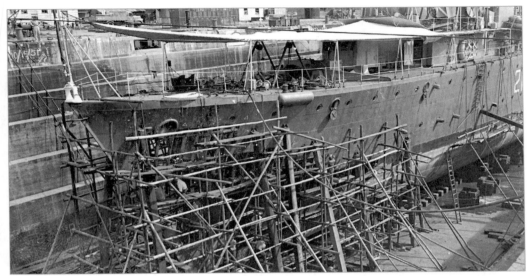

*HMCS* Huron *in dry dock at Sasebo, Japan, undergoing repairs for damage to her hull from her grounding accident, 1953.*

Huron's humiliation was not yet over. The damage was extensive; the ship remained in dry dock until October 25, almost three months after the armistice was signed. Sailors from other RCN ships were merciless in their taunting. One night the crew from one of them—purportedly *Iroquois*—hung a huge mural nearby showing a ship with her bow bent over a garden patch and the caption "The Invaders of the Rhubarb Patch…First to go ashore in North Korea, ship and all." For Commander Chenoweth and the two officers responsible for the grounding, it was even worse. Following a formal inquiry headed by then-Captain Landymore at Kure, Japan, all three were returned to Halifax, where they were court-martialled at *Stadacona* and given reprimands.

## ARMISTICE

THE KOREAN WAR ENDED a few days after *Huron*'s accident, on July 27, 1953, when an armistice was signed. Although largely eclipsed by the Canadian Army's participation in the war, the navy was first in and last out. Altogether, eight RCN destroyers and 3,621 sailors completed fifteen tours of duty in Korean waters before the armistice was signed. The Korean War was by far the most important conventional conflict of the Cold War years. The UN intervention in Korea marked the first time in history that an international organization had intervened effectively with a multinational force against aggression. More than fifty-five years later, the 250-kilometre border remains sealed, and Korean unification is perhaps further away than ever.

*The aircraft carrier* HMCS *Puncher arrives at Halifax, October 13, 1945.*

CHAPTER 10

# ABOVE AND BELOW

## THE REBIRTH OF NAVAL AVIATION

AFTER THE SUDDEN DEMISE of the Royal Canadian Naval Air Service in 1918, the RCN expressed an occasional interest in naval aviation between the two world wars, usually in the context of developments elsewhere. Meanwhile, the RCAF had been given the responsibility to conduct coastal patrols using shore-based maritime patrol aircraft. It took the Second World War to convince the Canadian government that naval air forces were an essential component of the war at sea.

When naval aviation returned to Dartmouth in September 1940, it was courtesy of the RN, which established a small base there. HMS *Seaborn* serviced RN aircraft and was a recruiting centre to enlist Canadians into the RN Fleet Air Arm. One of the Canadians

attached to the Fleet Air Arm, Lieutenant Robert Hampton "Hammy" Gray of Trail, British Columbia, became the only member of the RCN to be awarded the Victoria Cross. In the closing days of the war, on August 9, 1945, he flew his Corsair fighter-bomber through heavy Japanese shore- and ship-based fire to drop a bomb on the ocean escort *Amakusa*, which sank. Gray lost his life in the attack. His Victoria Cross was the last one awarded during the Second World War and the last Canadian one to date.

Later in the war, the RCN proposed to establish a Canadian naval air service, modelled on the British one, which would concentrate on carrier-based operations, while the RCAF conducted coastal operations with shore-based aircraft. In early 1944, the RCN manned two British light escort-carriers, *Nabob* and *Puncher*, with the aircraft and air personnel provided by the RN. The experiment soon ended. Under Captain Horatio Nelson Lay,

*Lieutenant "Hammy" Gray, c.1943. Gray was the only member of the Canadian navy awarded the Victoria Cross. Shearwater's Hampton Gray Memorial Centre is named after him.*

*Nabob* was so badly damaged during a torpedo attack in the Barents Sea in August that the British decided it was not worthwhile to repair her. *Puncher*, under the command of Captain Roger Bidwell, was relegated to ferrying aircraft and bringing Canadian troops home once the war ended. Undeterred, the government authorized the transfer of two RN light fleet-carriers, *Warrior* and *Magnificent*, to the RCN, with the option of Canada buying the carriers at some future date.

During the last summer of the war, the RN started to form air squadrons from Canadians serving in the Fleet Air Arm and former RCAF pilots who had transferred to the RN to fight in the war in the Pacific. The four squadrons designated for Canadian service were 803 and 883 squadrons, equipped with Seafire Mark 3 fighters (the naval version of the famous Spitfire) and 825 and 826 squadrons, flying two-seater Firefly Mark 1 fighter-reconnaissance aircraft. Another five hundred Canadian sailors who had served in the RN as ground crew or ship personnel formed the basis of ships' companies.

In December 1945, more than four months after the war ended, the government approved the formation of a naval air branch within the authorized manpower ceiling of the RCN—some eleven hundred sailors out of a peacetime strength of ten thousand. As this was not enough to adequately man an aircraft carrier, four aircraft squadrons, and shore-based support, the decision hampered the development of Canadian naval aviation.

Another decision made at the time caused similar difficulties. The RCAF controlled the funding of all naval aviation shore-based facilities and supporting air services, such as major aircraft repair and maintenance, as well as air stores. In other words, much of the operational effectiveness of the navy's aviation branch depended on the whim of another service, the RCAF, which had not shown itself to be particularly enamoured of the idea of a second "air force" in Canada. In fact, many RCAF officers, including the chief of the air staff, did everything they could to sabotage naval aviation.

## THE WARRIOR SPIRIT

AS HMCS *WARRIOR* APPROACHED her new home port of Halifax on March 31, 1946, under the command of Captain Frank Houghton, her thirteen Supermarine Seafire XVs and nine Firefly Mark 1s of 803 and 825 squadrons flew off to the RCN Air Section at Station Dartmouth. Because of available manpower, 826 and 833 squadrons had been temporarily deactivated and their personnel attached to the other two squadrons. Cheering crowds lined vantage points along the harbour. The sound of sirens from ships dressed for the occasion greeted *Warrior* as she entered the port on that fine, sunny day and tied up in the dockyard. The golden years of Canadian naval aviation had begun.

But life for naval aviators on a base under RCAF control was difficult. Shortages of clothing for flight crew and other stores were common, and the hangars and accommodation

*The arrival of the aircraft carrier* HMCS Warrior *at Halifax, March 31, 1946.*

allocated to the navy at Dartmouth were substandard. Although much of their time was spent flying over water, no immersion suits were provided to aircrew. In fact, pilots had been cautioned to remove their ties before flying in case they came down in the ocean, to prevent being strangled by their neckwear as it shrank in the salt water. Only later did some pilots realize that they would succumb to hypothermia in the cold waters off Nova Scotia long before a shrinking necktie became a threat.

When it became obvious that the British winterization of living quarters aboard *Warrior* was inadequate, arrangements were made to transfer the ship to the West Coast and its milder winters. After brief service on the West Coast, *Warrior* arrived back in Halifax in March 1947. Her two squadrons, 803 and 825, had been formed into the 19th Carrier Air group (CAG) before she sailed. By now, the RCN's ambitious plan to man two light fleet-carriers was realized as totally impractical within the assigned manpower ceiling. Plans were made to return *Warrior* to the British and take over the slightly larger *Magnificent*, then undergoing refit in Belfast, Northern Ireland.

On May 15, 1947, 826 and 883 squadrons reformed at Dartmouth and eventually took over the Seafires and Fireflies previously flown by 803 and 825 squadrons and became the 18th CAG. The RCNAS's first fatality occurred on July 17, when a Firefly crashed into the ocean near Musquodoboit, Nova Scotia, killing the pilot and observer. In mid-February 1948, *Warrior* sailed to Belfast, where finishing touches were being put on her replacement prior to commissioning. *Warrior* was handed back to the RN, while her crew joined

*RCN Firefly aircrew receive a mission briefing at the RCN Air Section Dartmouth, late 1940s.*

*Magnificent.* Canada's first aircraft carrier had a short life as an RCN warship, but during that time excellent co-operation developed between the air personnel and the ship's company, producing the team spirit essential to effective flying operations.

## C'EST MAGNIFIQUE!

MAGNIFICENT—AFFECTIONATELY KNOWN AS "MAGGIE"—was a Majestic class light fleet-carrier built by Harland and Wolff in Belfast. She was laid down in 1942, launched in 1944 (six months after *Warrior*), and commissioned into the RN in 1946. On March 21, 1948, she was recommissioned into the RCN, on loan from the British. After workups around Britain, *Magnificent* arrived in Halifax on June 1 under decorated Second World War veteran Commodore "Hard Over" Harry DeWolf, with new Sea Furies and Fireflies of the 19th CAG embarked. Unlike *Warrior, Magnificent* incorporated various Canadian specifications, including for service in cold-weather operations.

Later that year, the navy finally won its battle with the air force over control of Dartmouth, when the Cabinet Defence Committee authorized its transfer to the RCN in September, an action the air force fought to the end. The RCN promptly commissioned the base as HMCS *Shearwater* on December 1. Its first commander was Acting Captain Fraser Fraser-Harris of Halifax. Despite its rundown condition and lack of facilities, the naval aviation branch had a home it could finally call its own. Unfortunately, bringing the base up to an acceptable standard consumed a disproportionate amount of the navy's time, money, and effort.

*Acting Captain Fraser Fraser-Harris takes the salute at the commissioning parade for HMCS* Shearwater, *December 1, 1948.*

*A formation of four RCN Grumman Avengers flies over the aircraft carrier HMCS Magnificent, October 4, 1950. The destroyer HMCS Huron follows in her wake, and will move out to the port quarter as plane guard during launching and recovery of aircraft.*

A new 18th CAG had been formed in November, consisting of 826 and 825 squadrons, flying respectively Firefly Marks 1 and 4 (later replaced with Mark 5s), while 803 and 883 squadrons made up 19th CAG, flying new Sea Furies. The navy had been working on replacing its two-seater Fireflies, which were difficult to maintain, limited in number worldwide, and not well-suited to all-weather, anti-submarine warfare (ASW) carrier flying. In April 1950, the navy got its wish and the government purchased seventy-five second-hand USN Avenger AS3 aircraft. The three-man Avenger was a proven, rugged, and easy-to-maintain aircraft, which could carry the newest ASW equipment, provide more flying hours, and had an improved operational capability. This purchase also marked a move away from the RN, operationally and logistically, towards the USN, which had the most highly developed naval aviation branch in the world. For carrier defence however—at least temporarily—the RCN stayed with a British fighter and replaced the Seafires with Hawker Sea Furies.

Right from the start, Maggie participated in a seemingly endless round of training exercises and cruises for the next nine years, usually sailing the Atlantic, but also venturing into the Pacific to show the Canadian flag. On March 20, 1949, an occurrence of collective insubordination took place aboard *Magnificent*, the last of an infamous series of "incidents," which had happened earlier aboard *Ontario*, *Athabaskan*, and *Crescent*. Senior officers were loath to term these incidents mutinies because of the scandal that entailed, but they did order an investigation. The subsequent report of the Mainguy Commission resulted in long-overdue improvements in general service conditions as well as in overall officer-sailor relationships throughout the RCN.

In mid-January 1951, the two air groups were again reorganized. By then, 18th CAG consisted of 826 and 883 squadrons, equipped with Avengers and Sea Furies respectively. Squadrons 803 and 825, flying Sea Furies and Fireflies (later Avengers), became part of 19th Support Air Group, renamed because it was shore-based. On May 1, all RCN air squadrons were renumbered within the Commonwealth numbering system to give them a Canadian identity. Squadrons 803 and 825 became 870 and 880, respectively, and 19th Support Air Group became 31st Support Air Group, while 883 and 826 squadrons became 871 and 881 as members of 30th CAG, vice 18th CAG. (In June 1954, the administrative organization of the air groups was abolished, as the squadrons were usually deployed separately.)

Later that year, the RCN formed No. 1 Helicopter Flight at *Shearwater* with three Bell HTL-4 helicopters, required for aerial ice reconnaissance and light utility duties aboard the icebreaker HMCS *Labrador* (chapter twelve). After this initial experience with rotary-winged aircraft and the arrival of sufficient Sikorsky HO4S Horse helicopters (whose delivery began in 1952), the RCN formed HS 50, its first anti-submarine helicopter squadron in 1955, using the Horse fitted with dunking sonar. Later employed aboard *Magnificent*, the marriage of these rotary-winged aircraft to fixed-wing ones provided the navy with a

*A "prang" (crash) of a Grumman Avenger on the flight deck of* HMCS *Magnificent, August 9, 1956.*

balanced and versatile ASW capability. That same year, other new aircraft began to arrive at *Shearwater*. In January, four T-33 Silver Star trainers—the navy's first jets—arrived to begin jet conversion training for thirty-nine used F2H3 Banshee all-weather jet fighters that were purchased from the USN to replace the Sea Furies.

The Banshees were allocated to VF 870 and VF 871 squadrons and intended for the more modern aircraft carrier *Bonaventure*—nicknamed "Bonnie"—when she arrived. They also had an important shore-based interceptor role in NORAD in conjunction with the less capable CF-100s flown by the RCAF. For a long time the Sidewinder-equipped Banshees were the only Canadian aircraft carrying air-to-air missiles. The next year, the first of one hundred Canadian-built, anti-submarine aircraft was delivered to the RCN. The CS2F Tracker was the modified Canadian version of an American design and replaced the Avengers. This increased the navy's interoperability with the USN, as the Tracker could be serviced at any USN location that operated the American version.

Maggie also took time out from training to conduct some important operational tasks. To resolve the Suez Crisis between Israel and its Arab neighbours, Canada's Minister of External Affairs Lester B. Pearson had suggested the formation of a UN peacekeeping force and interposing it between the belligerents. On December 29, 1956, Maggie left Halifax with 233 army vehicles and four RCAF Otters stowed on her deck, plus 406 soldiers and

*Sailors form up for "divisions" between parked Grumman Avenger aircraft aboard* HMCS Magnificent, *early 1950s.*

one hundred tons of stores below decks—Canada's contribution to the United Nations Emergency Force. When she arrived at Port Said, Egypt, she immediately off-loaded army personnel, vehicles, and stores to commence the first ever UN peacekeeping contingent. With her UN mission complete, Maggie's RCN service was almost over. On April 10, 1957, she sailed from Halifax and was paid off at Plymouth in June.

## A BONNIE LASS IS LAST

MEANWHILE, IN APRIL 1952, Cabinet had authorized the purchase and modernization of an aircraft carrier and the RN's light fleet-carrier *Powerful* was selected. Although launched in late 1943, *Powerful* had been laid up since the spring of 1946, when all work on her ceased. This meant the RCN would have the opportunity to modify the carrier to meet Canadian requirements, but it also meant that her hull and many of her fittings were already nine years old, and it would take another five years to complete her construction. Rather than retain the name *Powerful*, the navy decided to rename the carrier *Bonaventure*, after the tiny island bird sanctuary in the Gulf of St. Lawrence.

Work on *Powerful/Bonaventure* recommenced in 1952 and included an angled flight deck, which provided a longer landing run without sacrificing forward parking space and resulted in the removal of the ever-unpopular crash barrier. Other improvements were a steam catapult and a mirror landing sight to help eliminate human error during landings. HMCS *Bonaventure* was commissioned at Belfast on January 17, 1957, and arrived in Halifax on June 26. On her deck she carried a "top secret" experimental hydrofoil. Bonnie was the first RCN-owned carrier to incorporate Canadian-designed features and the first to embark Banshees and Trackers.

Like her predecessor, Bonnie participated in a busy round of training and exercises, including several with the ships of other NATO navies. Beginning in August 1963, Sikorsky Sea Kings replaced the Horses. Between April 1966 and August 1967, Bonnie underwent what was expected to be her mid-life refit. The initial eight-million-dollar estimate ballooned to more than seventeen million dollars, some of it due to unnecessary repairs to cabins and fixtures. The political firestorm that followed gave senior government opponents of naval aviation the opportunity to scuttle *Bonaventure*. When NDHQ announced Bonnie's retirement in September 1969, it caused another political scandal, coming so soon after the nine-million-dollar overrun for her overhaul.

*A formation of Banshee all-weather fighter jets from* VF 870 *Squadron over the aircraft carrier* HMCS Bonaventure, *late 1950s. A Tracker (left) and a Horse helicopter are on deck.*

Various reasons have been suggested for *Bonaventure*'s premature retirement, but the most widely accepted reason is that it gave the Trudeau government—never a strong supporter of Canada's military—the chance to drastically cut naval expenditures. Bonnie was paid off in 1970 and sold for scrap. Today her anchor and chain serve as a memorial in Halifax's Point Pleasant Park to CF members who lost their lives at sea in peacetime.

Whatever the reason, Bonnie's fate emasculated Canada's naval aviation. When the Banshee came to the end of its operational life in 1962, it was retired from RCN service after seven years of yeoman duty, leaving Canadian ships without any dedicated air defence assets. Once the Trackers—relegated to a shore-based role after Bonnie's decommissioning—were retired, it reduced the navy's air assets to helicopters operating off destroyers and frigates. After the unification and integration fiasco of 1968 (chapter thirteen), all aviation assets devoted to maritime use, whether shore- or ship-based, belonged to the air force, and naval aviation ceased to exist.

## THE SILENT SERVICE

SUBMARINERS ARE NOT LIKE other sailors; they are a different breed. Apart from those who serve on enormous nuclear submarines, their working and living conditions would be unacceptable to most people. The constant smell of diesel fumes, exhaust gases, and human odours circulate through the already stale air of extremely cramped spaces.

*Canada's first submarines,* CC1 *and* CC2, *were originally purchased by the premier of British Columbia in 1914.*

Canada's acquisition of her first submarines (traditionally called "boats" rather than ships, no matter what their size) was not unlike an adventure story out of *Boy's Own Annual*. On the eve of the First World War, two submarines were under construction in Seattle, Washington, for the Chilean government. When the agreement fell through, British Columbia Premier Sir Richard McBride bought them in a secret deal with their builder, because of public fears about a lack of naval defences on the West Coast. Under cover of darkness, the submarines slipped out of the shipyard and sailed to Esquimalt. The federal government subsequently ratified McBride's impulsive action and the submarines were commissioned into the RCN as *CC1* and *CC2* in August 1914.

The boats trained and cruised off the West Coast for three years before they were ordered to Europe. In June 1917, they set sail for Halifax along with their tender, HMCS *Shearwater*. Their eleven-thousand-kilometre journey through the Panama Canal marked the first time a warship flying the White Ensign had transited the recently opened waterway. It was a harrowing voyage, marked by rough seas, sweltering temperatures, and continuous breakdowns. When *CC1* and *CC2* arrived in Halifax, their engines were declared unfit for the transatlantic crossing. The submarines remained at Halifax until they were sold for scrap in 1920.

Canada's next two submarines were H class ones that were also built in the United States, at Quincy, Massachusetts. They were ordered by Britain, but the war ended when they were at Bermuda on their way overseas. In 1919, the RN gave them to the RCN as replacements for *CC1* and *CC2* and they were commissioned at Halifax in April 1921 as *CH-14* and *CH-15*. They were hardly used and were paid off on June 30, 1922, victims of the drastic budget cuts of that year. To the displeasure of local residents, they lay alongside the cruiser *Aurora* in the Northwest Arm for many years before being towed away for scrap in 1927.

Canada's third pair of submarines was also obtained under unusual circumstances. A few days after the war in Europe ended, the German U-boats *u-190* and *u-889*, large Type IXC/40 subs, surrendered to RCN ships on May 10 and 11, 1945. Built at Bremen in 1942 (*u-190*) and 1944 (*u-889*), they were immediately commissioned into the RCN for evaluation and testing. In January 1946, *u-889* was turned over to the USN and sunk during torpedo tests off New England the next year.

*u-190* met her end in a particularly poignant way. After extensive trials involving the firing of acoustic torpedoes while aircraft took pictures, she was secured alongside in Halifax. She deteriorated rapidly there, and in July 1947 was paid off so the navy could use the U-boat for target practice in an exercise named Operation Scuppered. After her hull was painted bright yellow with red stripes, *u-190* left Halifax with a skeleton crew aboard.

*u-190* was towed to a position off the Nova Scotia coast, over the very spot where she had sunk HMCS *Esquimalt* in April 1945, the last RCN casualty of the war (chapter five), where her crew were taken off. On October 21—a day marked throughout Commonwealth navies as Trafalgar Day—warships of the RCN as well as aircraft of 826 and 883 squadrons gleefully anticipated shelling and bombing their former enemy. A rocket attack by 826 Squadron Fireflies quickly eliminated the need for further attacks by Seafires, destroyers, and a frigate. Immediately after the Fireflies' rockets hit home, the U-boat's bows lifted into the sky, she settled by the stern, and quickly slipped below the waters. In the minds of many, *Esquimalt* and her crew had been avenged.

During the post-Second World War period, the RCN focussed almost exclusively on ASW operations in a NATO context. An essential component of ASW training for both naval and maritime air forces is the use of submarines to represent enemy boats. From the mid-1950s to the early 1960s, such target submarines were provided by the RN's 6th Submarine Squadron, which had up to three A class boats permanently stationed at Halifax at any given time. The RCN paid for their operating and maintenance costs, and provided about 180 sailors for submarine service with the RN, many of them in the 6th Squadron.

In his book on the Canadian submarine service, former submariner J. David Perkins quotes RCN Sub-Lieutenant Peter Haydon, who was among those who served in the British boats, in this case *Alderney*. After being deployed off Greenland as a barrier to

*The German submarine U-889 surrenders to Fairmile motor launch Q 117 of the RCN off Shelburne, May 13, 1945. She was immediately commissioned into the Royal Canadian Navy.*

Soviet subs during the Cuban Missile Crisis of 1962 (chapter eleven), Haydon returned to Halifax, "not to a hero's welcome but to be treated poorly once again because after two months at sea, we did not have 'regulation' haircuts and were thus asked to leave the *Stadacona* wardroom bar." The submariner officers had a "constant battle" with the Base Commander and his staff, some of it "self-inflicted." As Haydon recalled, "there wasn't a really good reason to add a periscope to the painting of the battle of Trafalgar [hanging in the Wardroom], and perhaps we did not have to emulate Russians in throwing glasses into the fireplace, and perhaps we should have been more prudent in leaving the nurses' residence in the early hours of the morning."

## A CANADIAN SUBMARINE SERVICE

THE RCN BELIEVED THAT IT needed its own submarines for operational reasons however, which included more than simply ASW training. It needed them to kill enemy submarines. As a result, by 1960 a Canadian submarine service had been approved, although the type of boat had not yet been selected. While nuclear-powered submarines would have been the best choice, their price tag was too steep; one nuclear-powered boat cost about the same as six conventional ones, the number the navy wanted. Due to cost, the Cabinet Defence Committee agreed to the purchase of only three submarines in March 1962. Largely due to political disagreements between Prime Minister Diefenbaker and President Kennedy, they were Oberon class submarines from Britain instead of newer-designed Barbel class American boats.

The submarines *Ojibwa*, *Onondaga*, and *Okanagan* were built at the RN's Chatham Dockyard in Britain and commissioned in September 1965, June 1967, and June 1968, respectively. Together, they formed the 1st Submarine Squadron based in Halifax. The three diesel-electric Oberons, or O-boats, which cost more than fifty million dollars, were considered the quietest non-nuclear boats in the world, even though their design dated back to 1946.

The boats were delivered with either the RN's Mark 8 or Mark 20 torpedoes, which were replaced with the USN's Mark 37 in late 1968, creating more living space aboard them. When the subs were built, they were expected to provide a minimum of twenty years' service, but in fact *Okanagan* was in service for thirty years, while *Ojibwa* and *Onondaga* lasted thirty-three years before being paid off. For their first decade of service the O-boats were used only as training submarines and were not up to full operational standards until they received a wide range of improvements in the 1980s. Eventually, Canada replaced the O-boats with newer British submarines at the turn of the century (chapter 13).

*One of Canada's three Halifax-based O-boats at sea.*

*RCN ships in the Halifax dockyard decorated for Christmas 1955. The icebreaker HMCS Labrador (chapter 12) displays an illuminated star.*

CHAPTER 11

# THE COLD WAR NAVY

## NAVAL EXPANSION

A T THE END OF THE SECOND WORLD WAR, demobilization of "wartime only" personnel followed as quickly as possible. People were tired from six long years of conflict and looked forward to peace and prosperity. Despite the peace, the government still had to consider the shape and size of the country's postwar armed forces. A return to the miniscule strength of the pre-war RCN was out of the question—Canada had an international reputation to maintain as a new "middle power"—and naval planners had already considered the issue while the war was being fought.

The initial postwar strength approved for the RCN was ten thousand sailors to man a balanced force of two aircraft carriers, cruisers, destroyers, and a reserve fleet. It did not take long for the government to rein in these plans, and within two years the RCN was reduced by 25 per cent to seventy-five hundred personnel and a smaller fleet of one aircraft carrier, a cruiser, and five destroyers. The Korean War (chapter nine) quickly and dramatically reordered the government's priorities, resulting in the approval for a navy of twenty thousand sailors and one hundred ships by 1954. It also brought a change in the navy's role to concentrate on anti-submarine warfare, a task that the RCN had made its own during the Second World War.

Given the past problems of relying on other countries—no matter how close—for warship construction, the Naval Board realized the need for an anti-submarine destroyer designed and built in Canada. The result was the St. Laurent class, the so-called "Cadillac" destroyers. Beginning with these vessels, for the ten-year period from 1953–54 to 1963–64 the RCN underwent a previously unimagined peacetime expansion. The number of its major warships grew steadily; it designed and built forty-one new ships and carried out major conversions to another thirty-three.

## THE "CADILLACS"

The programme for the commissioning of HMCS St. Laurent at Montreal, October 29, 1955.

THE ST. LAURENT CLASS DESTROYERS were the first warships entirely designed and constructed in Canada. Between 1955 and 1957, seven of these world-class destroyers entered service: *St. Laurent, Assiniboine, Fraser, Margaree* (the only one named after a Nova Scotia river), *Ottawa, Saguenay,* and *Skeena.* These were followed by thirteen similar ships between 1958 and 1964 that incorporated various improvements. The first of these were seven Restigouche class: *Restigouche, Chaudière, Columbia, Gatineau, Kootenay, St. Croix,* and *Terra Nova;* followed by four Mackenzie class: *Mackenzie, Qu'Appelle, Saskatchewan,* and *Yukon;* and finally two Annapolis class: *Annapolis* and *Nipigon.* These twenty warships—all named after Canadian rivers—impressed friend and foe alike with their state-of-the-art capabilities. They came into service in an amazingly short period of nine years and symbolized the unique identity of the RCN and its expertise in ASW.

These destroyers were built for the harsh conditions of the North Atlantic, an area that the RCN knew all too well. Besides superior seakeeping abilities, long range, and good sustained speed, the ships incorporated design mechanisms to control icing up, engine noise, and radioactive fallout. In an extraordinary break with the past, the captain commanded in action from an operations room rather than from the bridge, a decision that did not sit well with many traditionalists.

The ships were also a giant leap forward in crew comfort, something that the Americans were very good at, but which always seemed to be the very last consideration in ship construction for the British. With the St. Laurent class, the RCN surpassed the USN in looking after its sailors. The ships had comfortable bunks and bedding—with reading lamps, no less—to replace the centuries-old tradition of slung hammocks, plus large personal lockers, modern galleys serving food to central cafeterias, improved washrooms and heads, better lighting, and on-board laundry facilities, along with more refrigeration, freezer rooms, air-conditioning, and fresh water.

HMCS *St. Laurent*—"Sally the Second"—arrived in Halifax on November 5, 1955, under her first captain, Commander Bob Timbrell, who had been awarded the Distinguished Service Cross for his courageous actions during the Dunkirk evacuation in June 1940. In April 1957, *St. Laurent* sailed to Britain to see if she could impress RN officers. She did. During a tour by the Lords of the Admiralty in London, Timbrell overheard one Sea Lord ask, "Why couldn't the RN come up with a ship like this?"

## HELICOPTERS

THE RCN'S FIRST ANTI-SUBMARINE helicopter squadron, using dunking sonar that was lowered into the water from a hovering Sikorsky HO4S Horse helicopter, flew from HMCS *Magnificent* in 1955. The next major step forward in anti-submarine helicopter operations was a purely Canadian idea, when the RCN pioneered the marriage of helicopters and ASW-specialized destroyer escorts. Trialled on the wartime Prestonian class ocean escort HMCS *Buckingham* in 1956 and HMCS *Ottawa* in 1957, this radical combination soon proved to be a giant step forward in ASW operations. All the Cadillacs were eventually retrofitted to carry helicopters, except for the two Annapolis class vessels, which were the first RCN ships designed from the keel up to be capable of carrying helicopters.

A further refinement of ship-borne helicopter operations was the Canadian-designed Beartrap helicopter haul-down system. *Assiniboine* became the trial ship for this development in October 1963 at Halifax. For the next two years, *Assiniboine* searched out North Atlantic storms to test the system. Ultimately, the trials were successful, despite several close calls due to less than four metres' clearance between rotor blades and the hangar door. "Bones" became the first of her class converted to a helicopter-carrying destroyer, known as a DDH.

*A Sea King helicopter from VX 10 Squadron engages* Assiniboine's *Beartrap haul-down system during the 1963–65 trials.*

*The Halifax dockyard in the late 1950s, with several warships alongside as a flotilla steams seaward under the Angus L. Macdonald Bridge.*

With the purchase of the Sea King helicopter in 1963, the RCN led the world in destroyer-helicopter ASW operations. Other navies believed that only an aircraft carrier could provide a suitable platform for a nine-ton helicopter and that helicopters could not operate at night. Canadians proved them wrong on both counts. According to Lee Myrhaugen, a retired air force colonel and pilot who logged four thousand hours aboard Sea Kings, "The rest of the world stood back, awestruck with the notion of putting such a large helicopter aboard such a relatively small ship."

## THE CUBAN MISSILE CRISIS

WHEN THE PRESENCE OF SOVIET ballistic missiles on Cuban soil was confirmed by photographic evidence from American aerial reconnaissance assets on October 13, 1962, the RCN and USN had already been co-operating in operations against Soviet naval activity in the western Atlantic since the early 1950s. A bilateral plan for the defence of North America had existed since 1946, and the naval staffs in Halifax and Norfolk, Virginia, as well as the warships and aircraft under their command, were used to working with each other.

At the beginning of October, Canadian and American ASW forces noticed that the pattern of activity of Soviet submarines, electronic intelligence "fishing" trawlers, and surface ships off the eastern seaboard had changed. Four days after the missile silos were

*The Halifax-built Tribal class destroyers (L–R)* Athabaskan, Nootka, Micmac, *and* Cayuga *alongside in Halifax, July 9, 1962, a few months before the Cuban Missile Crisis shook the world.*

photographed in Cuba, the admiral in charge of the USN's ASW assets and his aviation commander flew to Halifax from Norfolk for "discussions of immediate operational concern" with Rear Admiral Ken Dyer, the RCN's Flag Officer Atlantic Coast.

By then the Americans had already placed their forces on a heightened state of readiness, especially the ships and aircraft of the USN, and they hoped Canada would do the same. Dyer had five escort squadrons at his disposal. The 1st Escort Squadron, made up of older Tribal class destroyers, was in British waters in the company of *Bonaventure*. The Bonnie's Banshee jet fighter squadron had only been disbanded on September 30, considerably weakening her offensive capabilities and leaving her equipped only with Tracker patrol/reconnaissance aircraft and helicopters.

Dyer's other warships were in the 5th Escort Squadron, consisting of Restigouche class destroyers, as well as in the 7th and 9th escort squadrons of older Prestonian class vessels. All three squadrons were either at sea or in Halifax at short notice to move. Technically, the fifth and last of his escort squadrons, the 3rd at Halifax, was not readily available as it was made up of old destroyers and was on reduced manning. Dyer also controlled the RCAF's East Coast maritime patrol squadrons and two British training submarines assigned to him and based at Halifax. The latter could only be deployed operationally at a higher state of alert. All of the navy's St. Laurent class destroyers were on the West Coast, where they formed the only active squadron there, the 2nd.

United States President John F. Kennedy's confrontational speech on October 22 let the cat out of the bag, catching the Canadian as well as the American public by surprise. The bellicose tone of his speech left no doubt in the minds of Soviet leader Nikita Khrushchev and the rest of the world just how seriously the United States took this incursion into the western hemisphere, a region regarded as vital to America's interests since the enunciation of the Monroe Doctrine in 1823. Kennedy demanded an unconditional withdrawal of all Soviet missiles from Cuba and set up a quarantine zone around Cuba—in effect a blockade—to prevent any further shipments of military equipment to the island nation.

By the time of Kennedy's address to the world, Dyer had already reacted to the Soviet threat and taken considerable measures, including an increased state of alert. His Halifax-based ships had made their first contact with a Soviet submarine 480 kilometres off the Canadian coast on the night of October 17, to be followed by eleven more such contacts during the next three weeks.

Once President Kennedy made his speech, the American government began pressuring Prime Minister John Diefenbaker to raise the alert state of the Canadian Armed Forces and deploy ships and aircraft in support of the Cuban blockade. Diefenbaker, never on the friendliest terms with either the Americans or his own military, demurred. He and several of his cabinet ministers remained unconvinced of the seriousness of the threat and the need to move to a higher state of alert.

*The Halifax-based Prestonian class ocean escorts* HMC *Ships* Victoriaville, Inch Arran, *and* New Waterford *of the 7th Canadian Escort Squadron steam in line formation while on patrol off the East Coast of Canada during the Cuban Missile Crisis.*

Fortunately (or unfortunately in the view of some analysts), the RCN undertook additional security measures on its own, convinced that these actions were well within the standing authority of naval commanders for the defence of North America. On October 24, Ottawa's Naval Board approved the redeployment of *Bonaventure* and the 1st Escort Squadron from Britain and allowed Dyer to go to a higher state of readiness. Doug Prentice was a radio operator in *Athabaskan* at the time, moored at the dockyard in Plymouth, England, when the message came in from Dyer ordering them back to Canada immediately. "I can still remember the shudder of fear that overcame me," he recalled in a letter to *Legion Magazine* in 2009.

Within the hour, *Athabaskan* was underway. Her voyage to Halifax took only five days, despite encountering a hurricane. A day out of Halifax, *Athabaskan* steamed alongside *Bonaventure*. Prentice noted that the storm had crumpled the front end of her flight deck and many windows on the bridge were covered with plywood. He remembered thinking, "Is this just the start of World War Three?" The tension on board was palpable. Prentice feared that if the situation did not calm down "Halifax would probably not be there for long. I was one scared sailor."

Admiral Dyer's ships took up patrol areas off the coast of Nova Scotia and further afield. The 5th Squadron patrolled southeast of Halifax. Some of the ships of the 7th, which had been at sea, returned to Halifax, prepared for war, and deployed to Sydney for fuelling, while others remained on station. The 9th sailed to St. John's, Newfoundland, and set up a patrol area east of Cape Race, where it was supported by USN maritime patrol aircraft from the American base at Argentia. The 3rd was brought up to full manning and deployed to Shelburne to patrol the Georges Bank, while the two RN subs went to patrol areas on the northeastern edge of the Grand Banks.

Maritime aviation assets of the RCN and RCAF assisted the warships. Shearwater-based Trackers began coastal patrols and a detachment deployed to Sydney to help in the Cabot Strait area, while RCAF Argus patrol aircraft supported the 5th Squadron on the Georges Bank. Before these deployments occurred, USN naval and maritime air resources were already at a heightened state of alert. USN anti-submarine ships had established a barrier line southeast of Newfoundland, along the path of the SOSUS underwater acoustic sensors. RCAF maritime patrol aircraft supported this barrier operation. The USN asked the RCN to extend its patrols further south, as the bulk of American forces were involved in the blockade around Cuba. Although Dyer agreed, he did it on his own authority in the absence of any clear direction from either his political or naval masters in Ottawa.

For some reason, neither the politicians nor Vice Admiral Herbert Rayner, the chief of naval staff, were convinced that the Soviet subs posed a threat, despite the fact that American forces and their own were essentially on a war footing. Dyer was operating on "by exception" rules: he would signal his intentions to Ottawa and, in the absence of any objections or different direction, went ahead with his plans. In effect, the prime minister, his cabinet, and the head of the navy totally ignored their responsibilities to the nation, either through ignorance, incompetence, paralysis, or a combination of these. Whatever the reason, it was an inexcusable reaction to one of the most dangerous crises of the Cold War and the most serious threat to North America during that period.

To the public, the crisis ended on October 28, when Khrushchev apparently backed down and Soviet warships heading to Cuba turned around. But for the ships and sailors from Halifax, little seemed to have changed. The high level of Soviet submarine activity in their zone of responsibility continued unabated. On November 5, Dyer's force was at its peak deployment; Bonnie, twenty-four destroyers, and two British subs were spread across an area sixteen hundred kilometres long by four hundred kilometres wide. Submarine contacts continued until November 15, by which time 136 Soviet subs had been detected in or near the Atlantic Canadian zone.

All in all, it had been one of the most bizarre episodes in Canadian history. Fortunately, while the senior leadership in both the Canadian government and the navy did not seem to be prepared to do their sworn jobs in defending their country's sovereignty, others who clearly recognized the threat understood their responsibilities and carried out their duties.

## HMCS *SCOTIAN*

NAVAL RESERVISTS—like their regular force counterparts—were active during the Cold War. Back in March 1943, HMCS *Haligonian* had been commissioned as the Halifax Naval Reserve Division and assumed the duties previously performed by the Halifax Half Company. Its main task, however, was as a recruiting centre until the end of the war, when it was a final discharge centre for the thousands of sailors who were demobilized in Halifax. After the war, in 1946, *Haligonian* was paid off. Meanwhile, in June 1944, the dockyard was removed from the jurisdiction of the commanding officer of HMCS *Stadacona* and commissioned as a separate establishment, HMCS *Scotian*, under the commodore superintendent of the dockyard. When the year ended, *Scotian* administered the huge reserve fleet and numerous auxiliary vessels until it was paid off on February 28, 1947.

Two months later, on April 23, a new Naval Reserve Division was commissioned in Halifax, perpetuating the name HMCS *Scotian* and under the command of Captain W. E. S. Briggs, who had won the Distinguished Service Cross during the war. *Scotian* commenced training in its new home, H block in the dockyard. At the time, *Scotian* benefitted from having one or more tenders assigned to her, which greatly facilitated sea training.

In 1951, *Scotian* was assigned a new Cold War role: seaward defence. In 1954, the new minesweeper HMCS *Quinte* was allocated to *Scotian*, which made her at the time the only Naval Reserve Division that boasted an operational minesweeper. The highlight of the

*Reservists at* HMCS Scotian, *Halifax's Naval Reserve Division, undergo navigational instruction from a Stadacona rating.*

year for *Scotian's* reservists was summer training aboard the navy's warships. Not only were they learning from the professionals, they got to go to sea—and receive pay for it.

In 1958, *Scotian* moved again, to F Block in *Stadacona*. Four years later, these quarters had to be abandoned because of two separate fires occurring only months apart. New accommodation was in the Seaward Defence Establishment near Point Pleasant Park. A couple of years later, unit members were shocked to learn that *Scotian* was to be decommissioned as part of the government's austerity drive. A concerted appeal by concerned sailors and citizens resulted in a reprieve and on February 25, 1964, the unit received the welcome news that their division would remain in commission. A paying-off mess dinner scheduled for three nights later was quickly transformed from a wake to a celebration.

During Canada's centennial year, the Seaward Defence Establishment was turned over to the National Harbours Board and *Scotian* moved again, this time to the former RCAF Station Gorsebrook on South Street. While at Gorsebrook, *Scotian* continued to grow and became the one of the largest reserve divisions in the country. The next year it was awarded the "Silver Destroyer," the Naval Reserve's annual award of excellence. In 1985, *Scotian* moved into its present quarters, a purpose-built facility just south of the dockyard.

HMCS *KOOTENAY* WAS THE THIRD of the Restigouche class destroyers to be commissioned and arrived in Halifax in 1959. Ten years later, *Kootenay* had just completed an exercise off Britain with a task group consisting of the aircraft carrier HMCS *Bonaventure* and seven other destroyers when disaster struck.

On the morning of October 23, 1969, about 320 kilometres from Plymouth, England, the task group was heading westward to Halifax. At 6:05 the task group commander ordered *Kootenay* and *Saguenay* to separate from the group to carry out full power trials. *Saguenay* had already completed her task when *Kootenay* commenced hers at about 8:10. Commander Neil Norton passed the order "Full Ahead–Both Engines" to the engine room, manned at the time by ten engineering crew.

In his article, "HMCS *Kootenay* Gearbox Explosion," on the Canadian Navy of Yesterday and Today portion of the website "Hazegray & Underway," naval researcher Sandy McClearn, who has studied the *Kootenay* explosion extensively, details what happened next. In response to the order, "the throttles on both port and starboard turbines were opened up" and quickly "reached maximum revolutions, in the range of 5,750 RPM, and the main reduction gearboxes transferred power to the propeller shafts."

*A Sea King helicopter from one of the ships in the task group prepares to land firefighting equipment on* Kootenay's *quarterdeck following the explosion in the engine room of the destroyer escort on October 23, 1969.*

At 8:21, "the temperature in the starboard gearbox reached a critical level (estimated at 650 degrees C) and the gearbox exploded," hurling "a fireball forward in the engine room and up through the engine room hatches into the main flats (main fore-aft passageway), also named Burma Road." As thick, black smoke filled the ship, "orders were given to close the throttles and evacuate the engine room." But there was a problem. "Due to flames from the gearbox, the aft hatch was inaccessible, and flames were being directed towards the forward hatch by the circulation fans." Six of the engine room crew were killed instantly, while "four managed to escape via the forward hatch," including the engineering officer, Lieutenant Al Kennedy. One of the four died at the top of the hatch and the others suffered severe burns. Kennedy staggered to the bridge, reported on the explosion, and said that "the emergency shut-offs in the flats had to be activated immediately to stop the flow of steam" from the boilers to the engines, which were still running. Then he collapsed.

According to McClearn, "despite the explosion, and the closing of the turbine throttles, both turbines (now unmanned) were still receiving steam from the boiler room and the ship was charging ahead at full speed." Additionally, "the steam-driven lube oil circulating

*Stokers inspect damage in* Kootenay's *engine room after the fire was put out and the area cooled down.*

pump in the starboard gearbox was still working, and continued feeding the flames with oil." The wheelhouse, located below decks, "filled with smoke and had to be abandoned... leaving the ship out of control until the emergency helm station could be manned." To worsen matters, the "steam-driven electrical power generator, and main source of ship's power, was knocked out of commission by the explosion" and its backup diesel generators were not set up to start automatically if the main power failed, disrupting ship-to-ship communications during a critical period.

McClearn noted that once crewmen manually started the diesel generator, restoring power to the ship, *Kootenay* sent out a radio message at 8:36, "stating her emergency and requesting assistance." *Saguenay*'s Sea King helicopter, which was already airborne, flew to *Kootenay* immediately and "ended up ferrying equipment, supplies, and personnel from other ships in the task group." A few minutes later, "the fire was at its height," heating up the bulkhead of the after gun magazine and threatening to blow up the ammunition stored there. With seven dead and several more "incapacitated by burns or smoke inhalation," remaining crew members struggled to move ammunition away from the bulkhead, hose it down, and fight the fire. As the aft generator had not yet been started, the aft fire pump was not running. Along with reduced water pressure and a shortage of firefighting equipment, this hindered the efforts of the crew.

At 9:00, boiler room crew "were still at their posts shutting down the boilers" to reduce "the flow of steam to the engine room." By now, a bulge was expanding in the starboard

*Five members of* Kootenay's *ship's company who were treated in* HMCS Bonaventure's *sick bay for smoke inhalation.* (L–R) *Able Seaman Ken MacEachern, Petty Officer John Gregory, Corporal Russell Saunders, Leading Seaman Ashley Cheeseman, and Able Seaman Joseph Arimars.*

hull plates next to the burning gearbox, black marks scorched the hull, and smoke poured from vents. The fire gained ground over the next hour, "until an engineering rating was eventually found to start the aft generator," allowing the aft fire pump to operate.

By about 10:10, sailors succeeded in bringing the fire under control and finally put it out between 10:30 and 11:00. It was only then that crewmen could enter the engine room without being driven back by the intense heat. Powerless, *Kootenay* was rigged for tow and by 11:15 was under tow by *Saguenay*. Meanwhile, "the engine room was cooled down" and the grim tasks of "damage assessment and removal of the…bodies from the engine room began." It was bad. Besides the seven killed earlier, two other sailors died from smoke inhalation, one during the fire and the other later in Bonaventure. An additional fifty-three suffered injuries. The next day, an RN tug took over the tow from *Saguenay*, which continued to escort the stricken vessel to Plymouth, where *Kootenay* went into dry dock. *Kootenay*'s propellers were removed and on November 16 the Dutch tug *Elbe* towed her to Halifax, arriving eleven days later.

A Board of Inquiry into the accident "concluded that insert bearing shells had been installed backwards in the starboard gearbox four years previously, which cut off the proper flow of lubricating oil, leading to overheating of the bearing and the ignition of the lubrication oil." The situation was compounded when the explosion killed or incapacitated a large part of the engine room crew, who were among the most experienced in damage control. Ultimately, the training of surviving crew members succeeded in overcoming the disastrous explosion and fire in *Kootenay*. In the words of Commander Norton, "A less professional crew could easily have finished the day in life rafts."

The incident had a profound effect on the navy's future firefighting and damage control training that is still felt today. As part of their education, sailors undergo training at a state-of-the-art firefighting school at Purcells Cove, near Halifax, where they fight fires and floods in realistic, ship-like conditions in a controlled environment: the Damage Control Training Facility Kootenay. As well, when the Canadian honours system was revamped in 1972, the first six bravery awards went to *Kootenay* sailors: two Crosses of Valour (both posthumous) out of only four awarded to date, two Stars of Courage, and two Medals of Bravery. *Kootenay*'s catastrophe was the worst peacetime accident ever in the Canadian Navy. The names of those who died in the accident are inscribed on the Bonaventure Memorial in Halifax's Point Pleasant Park.

*HMCS* Labrador *smashes through the sea ice during her epic 1954 transit of the Northwest Passage.*

CHAPTER 12

# NEW HORIZONS

## ICE QUEEN

DURING THE 1950S WHEN THE NUMBER OF RCN major warships increased steadily, it was clearly the right time to experiment with new and developing technologies. One of these involved a non-traditional vessel for the RCN—an ice-breaker. Sunday, November 21, 1954, was a typical fall day in Halifax. As high winds, fog, and rain greeted her, a ship sailed past Point Pleasant Park and into the history books. The icebreaker HMCS *Labrador* had returned home after one of the most momentous voyages in Canadian maritime history.

*Labrador*, her 246-man crew, and 23 National Research Council scientists had just sailed around the entire continent, having steamed almost twenty-nine thousand kilometres on her four-month voyage and established many records in the process. The next day, the front page of the Halifax *Chronicle Herald* proudly proclaimed *Labrador* "Back from Northern Conquest." And what a conquest it had been. At the helm of *Labrador* during her history-making cruise was now-Captain Long Robbie Robertson, the man who had twice saved Halifax from potentially devastating explosions during the Second World War.

The search for a sea route around the north of the Canadian mainland was an elusive goal not realized for more than four hundred years, consuming and frustrating genera-tions of explorers and leading to untimely death for many of them. A Northwest Passage was regarded as a direct, short route from the trading centres of northern Europe to the fabled wealth of the Far East. With the wartime transits of the passage by the 80-ton, wooden RCMP schooner *St. Roch* firmly in mind, the idea of a giant naval icebreaker was conceived in the 1940s as a way of asserting Canadian sovereignty, as well as conduct-ing scientific and hydrographic surveys, in the Arctic. Built in the MIL Shipyard at Sorel, Quebec, *Labrador* was commissioned on July 8, 1954. At 6,490 tons she was the largest and most complex naval ship ever built in Canada up to that time.

*Labrador* left Halifax on July 23, 1954, modified from a simple patrol vessel to an elabo-rately equipped floating laboratory, hospital, transport ship, rescue vessel, school, and explorer "extraordinaire" costing twenty million dollars. In typical Canadian fashion, her main armament, a twin 3-inch gun, was left in storage in Halifax. With minimal work-up time and only three of her officers trained in northern operations, *Labrador* crossed the Arctic Circle four and a half days after leaving Halifax. Her first meeting with ice occurred off Greenland, where floes 1.2 metres thick and over 400 metres long were encountered along with numerous icebergs, seen only by radar through impenetrable fog.

### ICE TEST

WHEN THE FOG LIFTED, the crew were astonished to see their ship surrounded by ice-bergs as far as the eye could see; icebergs of all shapes and sizes—new ones, massive and chunky, older ones, weathered and eroded. The sailors suddenly came to understand the fate of the *Titanic*. *Labrador*'s two Bell HTL-4 helicopters were dispatched ahead on an ice reconnaissance as the ship's six powerful diesel generators came on line, their combined twelve thousand horsepower propelling her forward under full power.

At the entrance to Lancaster Sound, *Labrador* had the first test of her builders' ability. As 6,500 tons of steel successfully smashed through the pack ice, cutting a swathe through the ice-filled sea, the crew breathed a collective sigh of relief. Their ship was a tough lady. Robertson next entered Lancaster Sound, breaking out of the ice and heading for the RCAF station at Resolute Bay where 405 Squadron, equipped with Lancaster bombers, was engaged in ice reconnaissance work. As the ship passed Devon Island, dark cliffs, capped by permanent ice cap, rose steeply three hundred metres straight out of the sea.

A radio message from the airmen at Resolute Bay welcomed the sailors to use "the north-ernmost flush-toilet system in the world!"

On August 1, the icebreaker dropped anchor off Resolute Bay, nine days and thirty-two hundred kilometres after leaving Halifax. It had not been the fastest of voyages, but it was a good one for a new crew on a new ship operating in a new environment. Among the many items off-loaded at Resolute was a 5.5-metre boat for the air force, built on Nova Scotia's Tancook Island. Hydrographers and other scientists, supported by naval person-nel, were disembarked to completely rechart Resolute Bay and its approaches. They stayed ashore for three weeks, while *Labrador* headed north to Ellesmere Island.

## FARTHEST NORTH

*LABRADOR'S* FIRST PORT OF CALL was the Inuit settlement and RCMP post at Craig Harbour on Ellesmere Island, where Inuit Special Constable Ariak, his wife Koono, four children, worldly goods, and seventeen half-wild huskies came on board, and then headed for Alexandra Fiord on Ellesmere Island. Further north in Smith Sound, *Labrador* encoun-tered the heaviest ice to date—three-metre thick, tough, smooth polar pack ice. Progress through it was measured in metres as the ship was jarred and squeezed, ramming her way

*The pipe "Hands to goofing stations" meant something unusual could be seen from the upper deck; in this case walruses on an Arctic ice floe, August 12, 1954.*

through by charging the ice at high speed, running up on top of it and smashing through with her great weight. On the way, the first polar bear was sighted, far from shore out on the sea ice. "Follow that bear!" Robertson roared to the helmsman. As the ship pounded along in full pursuit, all hands gathered on deck to watch the chase. Before coming into camera range, the bear disappeared into a pool of open water. That night, the ship's newspaper, *Bergy Bits*, carried the headline "Bear Foils Ship."

At Alexandra Fiord, Ariak, his family, and dogs disembarked. The Chief Bosun's Mate or "Buffer" was happy to see them go, at least as far as the huskies were concerned. In an unguarded moment, one of the dogs ate a pair of his leather gloves, entailing an investigation into the loss of naval equipment belonging to Her Majesty. The waters of Alexandra Fiord, the RCMP's most northerly outpost at less than one thousand kilometres from the North Pole, were uncharted. As a result, *Pogo*, the icebreaker's charting and survey launch, was hoisted out and lowered into the water. She sounded ahead of *Labrador* as the icebreaker followed cautiously behind, dropping anchor when *Pogo*'s echo-sounder indicated the bottom was rapidly becoming shallow. *Labrador* had just established a record for sailing the farthest north of any RCN ship.

### "YOU LOAD FOURTEEN TONS..."

THE NEXT THREE DAYS were spent off-loading eighty tons of coal and enough food for the detachment for a year via the icebreaker's two landing craft. On the evening of the third day, the last of the coal, some fourteen tons, was all that remained to be taken ashore. As the crew struggled to load the remaining heavy bags into the landing craft, Robertson decided the ship's officers and chief petty officers would race against each other to deliver it, much to the delight of the weary sailors.

At the crack of a rifle shot and the loud cheers of the lower deck ratings, the two landing craft raced towards the shore, almost five kilometres away. Twelve officers and twelve chief petty officers ran neck and neck to the beach—dodging ice floes all the way—dropped their ramps and unloaded seven tons of coal each in fifteen minutes. As the crews jumped back into their landing craft, the ramp on the officers' vessel jammed in the half-closed position. By the time they got it fixed, the chiefs' lead was unbeatable and they won the race by fifteen seconds. Their prize was a tin plate engraved "Presented by the Ellesmere Island Jockey Club."

### NEW MISSION

HER TASKS AT ALEXANDRA FIORD finished, *Labrador* returned to Resolute with her assigned Arctic mission complete. Rumours were rife among the crew as to what would happen next; would the captain sail westwards or return to Halifax? What was his plan? A very cunning one, as it turned out. On a Friday night Robertson sent a message to Naval Headquarters, just after everyone had gone home. It read:

> *"From Labrador to Naval HQ Ottawa*
> *Primary role completed*
> *Returning to Halifax via Esquimalt and Panama Canal."*

As *Labrador* steamed slowly westwards through the ice, a return message arrived. Permission had been received to proceed and establish contact with an American naval expedition in the Western Arctic, and then make for Esquimalt. The crew were ecstatic, despite the captain's grave warnings of the dangers involved with thick ice before the distant West Coast port would be reached. At the end of August, 405 Squadron made a final drop of mail and supplies, including spare parts for the ship's radar that had been down for a few days. As luck would have it one parachute failed and the much-needed radar spares were smashed beyond recognition, while a birthday cake landed with every decoration in place.

## RECORD TRANSIT

AFTER CONDUCTING A JOINT expedition with two American ships, *Labrador* turned southwest on September 20. She was the first warship in history to transit the elusive and forbidding route, and only the third ship ever to do so. *Labrador*'s voyage clearly showed

*Scientists from HMCS* Labrador *conduct experiments on the ice during her 1954 Arctic voyage.*

*A Piasecki HUP-3 helicopter leads two Bell HTL-4 helicopters past an iceberg off HMCS* Labrador *during her 1955 voyage to the Arctic.*

the need for charting virgin territory and correcting existing charts of the North. At one stage during her transit, a badly outdated chart said the ship was sailing over a twelve-hundred-metre mountain.

When the record-making icebreaker arrived in Esquimalt on September 27, her once pristine white paintwork weather-beaten and rust-streaked, she received a hero's welcome and was mobbed by the public and the press. In Robertson's words, *Labrador* had "accomplished every objective that had been set for it." *Labrador* sailed for warmer climes on October 15, transiting the Panama Canal on her way to Halifax. On November 23, after a voyage of 122 days, 97 of which were at sea, her journey came to an end. The first ship to complete a continuous circumnavigation of North America was home.

Robertson returned to the North in *Labrador* in 1955 and left the icebreaker the next year. He continued to be involved in Arctic developments however, and made several northern voyages in USN nuclear submarines. On one such trip he claimed to have organized the first baseball game at the North Pole, which also witnessed a few other "firsts." "The pitcher and the batter, of course, were facing each other," he recalled, "but both were facing north. Then, the first batter knocked a pop fly on Sunday morning, and the first baseman caught him out on Monday morning! The ball had crossed the dateline."

## FINAL DAYS

LABRADOR'S HULL NUMBER "50" was a familiar sight in the Arctic during further deployments in the mid-1950s. As well as establishing many more record-setting firsts, she accomplished additional survey and charting tasks and scientific achievements. *Labrador*'s exploits proved that large, deep-draft ships could navigate the Northwest Passage.

*In 1978, Canada Post issued a four-stamp set featuring ice vessels, one of which depicted HMCS* Labrador *during her 1954 Arctic voyage.*

Unfortunately, *Labrador* remained an RCN ship for only a short period of time. In 1957, the government decided she was no longer needed as a navy asset and turned her over to the Canadian Coast Guard. She did yeoman service in Coast Guard colours before finally being paid off in Halifax in 1987 and sold for scrap. Robertson, then retired, was among those gathered to say farewell to the old workhorse, known as "the Forgotten Fifty" to the sailors who crewed her. The Queen of the Ice was no more.

## FLYING ON WATER

ANOTHER NON-TRADITIONAL VESSEL built for the RCN was based on research and development that had been done on Cape Breton Island a half-century earlier—a hydrofoil. Within the space of fifty years, Canadian hydrofoil boats established two world records. At Baddeck, Alexander Graham Bell and his young collaborator "Casey" Baldwin set a watercraft speed record of 61½ knots on September 9, 1919, in their hydrofoil boat *HD-4*. Fifty years later, on July 9, 1969, HMCS *Bras d'Or* became the world's fastest warship with a speed of sixty-two knots, only slightly more than *HD-4*'s.

Seemingly by sheer chance, Nova Scotia became the site of some of the most advanced technological testing and experimentation with hydrofoils in the world. The record-setting private enterprise of Bell and Baldwin became the earliest sustained hydrofoil experiment in history. Their work gave way to a series of RCN projects in

*Bell and Baldwin's giant hydrofoil* HD-4 *broke the world watercraft speed record on September 9, 1919, on Cape Breton's Bras d'Or Lakes.*

mid-century, based at Halifax, which lasted nearly twenty-five years. Regrettably, both undertakings eventually suffered the same unfortunate fate when it came to commercial development.

## BELL AND BALDWIN

IT TOOK BELL AND BALDWIN eleven long years of trial and error, high hopes and dashed dreams, exceptional insights and false leads to achieve their extraordinary success with HD-4. Baldwin referred to the hydrofoil as "The Cigar"—a long, sleek, torpedo-shaped giant, years ahead of its time. After HD-4's launching, Bell invited Washington and Ottawa to send naval observers to her trials. In response, a lowly RCN lieutenant showed up on Christmas Eve 1918 to witness a preliminary test. From the first, HD-4 lifted easily onto her hydrofoil blades, clearing the water quickly, and once up accelerated rapidly to top speed in a smooth, gentle ride.

When the navy did not make any commitment to HD-4's development, Baldwin decided to test her potential as a target. In September 1921, the destroyer HMCS *Patriot* assisted in high-speed towing trials with HD-4, which RCN officers deemed successful. Bell subsequently offered HD-4's hull to the navy for towing targets; surprisingly, officials declined. Bell beached her on the shore of his estate, Beinn Bhreagh. Undeterred, Baldwin took a new approach and in 1920 started designing hydrofoils to carry towed naval targets. As these trials did not result in any immediate commitments, Baldwin turned to other areas. When the Second World War broke out, he returned to towed hydrofoil targets and designed several for the armed forces.

*HMCS* Patriot *tows a stripped-down* HD-4 *across the Bras d'Or Lakes in one of several target-towing experiments, 1921.*

## DUNCAN HODGSON

THE TWO PERIODS OF major hydrofoil development in Nova Scotia are connected by Lieutenant Commander Duncan Hodgson of the RCNR. Hodgson was not like most other naval officers—he was rich. During the Second World War, his family loaned their spacious Montreal townhouse to the local RCNVR unit as a headquarters and modest overnight accommodation for its members. Now that the war was over, he was bored and looking for excitement. Perhaps the Explorers Club in New York, of which he was a member, or Phil Rhodes, his old yacht designer friend and Baldwin's collaborator on hydrofoil motorboats, could come up with some ideas. Recalling his wartime experience working on a smoke-generating hydrofoil designed by Baldwin for the army, Hodgson remembered how exhilarating piloting the small, fast craft had been. He decided to commission Rhodes to design a hydrofoil boat for him to attack the world speed record. Rhodes readily agreed.

Word soon spread about what Hodgson was up to. When El Davies, vice-chairman of the newly established Defence Research Board (DRB) and an acquaintance of Hodgson, became aware of his friend's hydrofoil plans, he persuaded Hodgson to design instead a vessel to show the naval potential of hydrofoils. In late 1947, Hodgson's efforts convinced Davies of the hydrofoil's potential and he recommended DRB and the RCN become involved. As a result, the navy recalled Hodgson to active duty as project officer and attached him to DRB to develop a hydrofoil design for demonstration purposes.

Rhodes modified his hydrofoil design for naval use and submitted it to Davies at DRB in 1948, which applied the designation *R-100* to the project. Over the next few years, Hodgson's idea led to the development of an indigenous Canadian hydrofoil ship, an extraordinary vessel that captured the attention of the world's navies before suffering a strikingly similar fate to Bell and Baldwin's record-setting *HD-4*.

## MASSAWIPPI

DRB AWARDED THE CONTRACT to build *R-100* to McCrea's Boat Shop on Lake Massawippi in Quebec's Eastern Townships in June 1949, leading to her second name, *Massawippi*. Although several minor problems plagued her construction, *Massawippi* was completed in January 1950. The fourteen-metre, 5-ton, plywood craft did not have a cabin or superstructure and resembled a conventional motorboat. Before her completion, a committee chaired by Davies to monitor *Massawippi*'s construction decided Halifax would be the best location for testing. In February 1950, a series of rough-water trials began from the dockyard with Hodgson, now a commander, at the helm.

Hodgson kept a car in Halifax for his visits there, the height of affluence to others on the project struggling on minimum salaries. In Halifax the "secret" craft received her third name. In honour of Casey Baldwin's work, staff painted the letters *KC-B* on her sides, although her original unofficial name—*Massawippi*—prevailed throughout her lifetime. Then, towards the end of 1951, research engineers decided to design a hydrofoil similar to *Massawippi* but capable of meeting naval needs to tie in with current British research.

*Based on an idea of Lieutenant Commander Duncan Hodgson,* Massawippi *skims across the surface of Halifax Harbour.*

Initially designated *R-103*, but confusingly launched as *Bras d'Or* and later renamed *Baddeck*, she was built in Wales.

## THE FIRST *BRAS D'OR*

THE BIG MOMENT FOR the world's newest hydrofoil, *Bras d'Or*, finally arrived on Wednesday, May 22, 1957—foilborne trials off Wales. Pete Payzant, a Halifax engineer, had been sent to observe the trials. In a letter to his wife, Joan, he described what happened: "An attempt was made to get the boat foilborne and it failed miserably. Just before reaching expected foilborne speed, the boat started rolling rather alarmingly and the trial was curtailed." Unfortunately, engineering problems and delays plagued *Bras d'Or* throughout her construction, delaying her delivery for three and a half years.

When *Bras d'Or* was ready, she was transported to Halifax aboard HMCS *Bonaventure*, the aircraft carrier Britain sold to Canada, which was then undergoing completion at shipyards in Belfast (chapter ten). Finally completed in January 1957 after several delays, in her first task after acceptance trials *Bonaventure* solved the problem of getting *Bras d'Or* to

*The first hydrofoil* Bras d'Or *up on her foils in Bedford Basin. She later was renamed* Baddeck *when* HMCS Bras d'Or *was constructed.*

Canada. She carried her on the flight deck, shrouded in canvas and, supposedly, secrecy. When Bonnie arrived in Halifax on June 26, 1957, the local press had a field day over her "secret" cargo as they informed their readers what it was.

## THE LAST *BRAS D'OR*

EXTENSIVE TRIALS IN HALIFAX HARBOUR indicated that a rearrangement of *Bras d'Or*'s foils—in effect a complete reversal of their original configuration—would prove much more effective and provide the essential stability that had been missing up to then. Based on this assessment, in April 1961, DRB approved development of a preliminary design for a 180-ton hydrofoil ship for open-ocean use; it was to be known as a fast hydrofoil escort. Confusingly, she was christened *Bras d'Or*, while the original *Bras d'Or* was renamed *Baddeck*, maintaining the connection with Bell and Baldwin's experiments on Cape Breton Island.

*Bras d'Or*, carrying hull number 400 and with her superstructure and hull painted a sea grey above a scarlet bottom and foils, left the MIL Shipyard at Sorel on a slave dock on July 13, 1968, towed by navy tugs. It had taken seven years to get this far. Part of the delay was self-imposed because of frequent and substantial design changes; a full year was due to a disastrous November 1966 fire that set the ship's construction back. High hopes attended her arrival in Halifax, four days after her departure; the local press touted it as Canada's "first, futuristic and costly hydrofoil anti-submarine ship." The normal ship's company for *Bras d'Or* consisted of only twenty-three sailors, including her captain and four other officers—executive, engineering, navigation, and weapons. Six petty officers and a dozen seamen made up the rest of her complement.

## FOILBORNE!

AT MIDDAY ON WEDNESDAY, APRIL 9, 1969, hydrofoil history was about to be made once again in Nova Scotia waters, just as Bell and Baldwin had done a half-century earlier. Canada's innovative—and expensive—new warship left her Halifax berth that cool, sunny morning, accompanied by a frigate and various small craft with naval photographers aboard. The ship, her captain, his crew, and the contractors were ready, but anxious. So much of the ship's young life to date had been filled with disappointment and failure—would this day be any different?

The religious folk aboard whispered silent prayers. Failure was bad enough, but far worse in full view of others while being recorded for posterity by cameras. In contrast to virtually every other ship in the navy, *Bras d'Or*'s captain and helmsman actually "drove" their ship because the hydrofoil's tiny bridge had spaces for only three of her crew: the captain, coxswain, and navigator. Commander Tino Cotaras and Chief Sonarman Chief Petty

*A spectacular aerial photograph of* HMCS Bras d'Or *foilborne at speed.*

Officer Barry Howles were strapped into bucket seats beside each other, sitting at twin helms resembling an airplane's flight deck, while the navigator, Lieutenant Mike Hodgson, squeezed his bulk into the tiny jump seat behind them across from a small chart table.

Arriving at the test area off Chebucto Head at the entrance to the outer harbour, Cotaras and Howles glanced nervously at each other, and then cautiously advanced the throttles, pushing the ship up to her maximum hullborne speed of fourteen knots while they brought her muscular twenty-two thousand horsepower gas turbine engine into play. At 2,500 RPM, *Bras d'Or* leapt easily up onto her foils and screamed across the water at thirty-five knots, trailing mist, spray, and a faint stream of black smoke. Foilborne! Elated at having achieved their first "flight," the ship's company and contractors whooped and hollered in sheer joy, and then breathed a collective sigh of relief. It almost made all their hard work and the long wait, with all its troubles, worthwhile.

## CRACKS APPEAR

SHORTLY AFTERWARDS, the first indication of problems that would plague *Bras d'Or* began to surface, when technicians noticed saltwater seepage inside some of the foils. On July 18, 1969, *Bras d'Or* went into dry dock for the leaks to be repaired, and the findings shocked everyone. The first of several cracks were found in various foils, including the centre high-speed one. Technicians could fix the others, but not the high-speed foil.

*HMCS* Bras d'Or *on a floating dry dock at Halifax. When cracks developed in her complicated foil system, it spelled the end of the world's fastest warship.*

These problems eventually led to the hydrofoil project's demise, but not before her second and last captain, the flamboyant Gordon Edwards, took her on a spectacular fourteen-day, four-thousand-kilometre voyage in June 1971 from Halifax to Bermuda, then on to Norfolk, Virginia, the headquarters of NATO's Supreme Allied Commander Atlantic, and then back to Halifax.

In the House of Commons that November, Defence Minister Donald Macdonald announced that *Bras d'Or* would be laid up for five years. The few naval and civilian personnel not already posted out began preparations to put her into storage. They flushed out her fluids, sealed her systems, and coated her circuits. Partway through the preservation process, the hydrofoil underwent formal decommissioning in a simple ceremony on May 1, 1972.

In 1976, Macdonald's successor, James Richardson, announced *Bras d'Or* would be kept "in a state of preservation for a further five years until a final decision is made on the future of hydrofoils in the Canadian Forces." Then, the next year, the Vice Chief of the Defence Staff, Vice Admiral Bob Falls, recommended disposal. After a couple of Nova Scotia museums turned her down, in 1983 the Musée Maritime du Québec bought *Bras d'Or*. She sits on display today, high and dry on concrete pylons, a hole unceremoniously cut in her hull for visitor access. Like the Queen of the Ice, the world's fastest warship was no more.

*Led by an operational support ship and two destroyer escorts, a portion of the Canadian fleet exercises at sea. Canada possesses one of the finest small navies in the world.*

## CHAPTER 13

# UNIFICATION AND AFTER

### INTEGRATION AND UNIFICATION

IN THE OPINION OF MANY PEOPLE, one of the greatest frauds ever perpetrated on Canadians took place more than forty years ago. The three separate services of the armed forces—the Royal Canadian Navy, Canadian Army, and Royal Canadian Air Force—ceased to exist on February 1, 1968, and passed into history. In their place was something new, the brainchild of Paul Hellyer, an aggressive and ambitious Liberal minister of national defence. Hellyer's creation was an amorphous organization called the Canadian Armed Forces. In many respects, the armed forces have never recovered from the profound damage caused by Hellyer's sweeping double whammy: integration and unification.

*On the navy's seventy-fifth anniversary in 1985, Canada Post issued a stamp depicting a 1910 gunner's mate, a Second World War officer, and a woman in modern dress.*

Integration—the amalgamation of support services—was not a new idea, nor was it necessarily a bad one. By 1963, when Hellyer became defence minister, medical, dental, legal, and chaplain resources had already been integrated. Some further integration made sense to eliminate duplication and waste. If he had stopped at integration, Hellyer would probably be remembered much more favourably than he is today. But integration alone would never catch the public imagination and propel him to prime minister, replacing Mike Pearson. Something more was needed.

Hellyer had an ally in the report of the Glassco Commission on government organization, which pointed out bottlenecks, administrative confusion, and duplication of effort in the Department of National Defence. His solution was unification—the replacement of the three separate services with one, under one Chief of Defence Staff. In March 1964, the Liberals tabled a white paper on defence, the single-handed creation of Hellyer. Buried in the detail was the formation of a "single unified defence force." When senior officers protested, Hellyer considered it the equivalent of mutiny. During the 1944 manpower crisis of the Second World War, the RCAF had unceremoniously unloaded Hellyer on the army, where he had had to repeat basic training. This lack of co-ordination and waste of time still annoyed him. Eventually, he got his revenge.

Hellyer moved swiftly. National Defence Headquarters was reorganized, new commands were formed. Navy shore establishments, army camps, and air force stations became Canadian Forces Bases. The RCN became Maritime Command, while the army was known as Mobile Command. The RCAF was broken into two groups—Air Defence Command and Air Transport Command. Training, Communications, and Material commands rounded out the reorganization. Over the years, this structure has been changed, but the navy remains Maritime Command. Senior officers, attempting the equivalent of changing a tire on a moving car, had little time to react. Few accepted Hellyer's main premises for unification. It could not alter the fact that much of the armed forces' work was accomplished in single service settings. But Hellyer, enamoured of words like "flexible" and "mobile," would not listen.

While common uniforms, badges of rank, and rank titles certainly Canadianized the armed forces, they did little more than demoralize sailors, soldiers, and airmen. In particular, Canadian sailors, who had worn the traditional dark blue of uniformed seamen around the world, now wore a very unseamanlike green. The square rig of junior ratings and the double-breasted round rig (known earlier as "fore-and-aft rig") of POs and officers coalesced into a common single-breasted tunic. Petty officers became sergeants and commanders became lieutenant colonels.

Several senior officers resigned, including from the most traditional of the services— the navy. One of them was Rear Admiral Bill Landymore, who had commanded *Iroquois* in Korea (chapter 9) and later rose to head Canada's East Coast fleet in Halifax as Flag Officer Atlantic Coast. While in command, he became the man most identified with leading resistance to unification by taking the whole question to the public. His efforts were largely responsible for making unification national news. After a bitter dispute, culminating in the so-called "Admiral's Revolt," Landymore was forced into early retirement in 1966.

The places of those who resigned were quickly filled by opportunistic individuals who, like Hellyer, saw unification as a way to make their mark. Outside the armed forces, unification never became a major concern for most Canadians. When the opposition Conservatives finally seized on it as an issue, they subjected Hellyer's reorganization bill to criticism and delays. It only passed with the imminent closure of Parliament in April 1967.

Suddenly, Hellyer's path to replace Pearson was decidedly bumpy. He wanted a less controversial department. By the time unification became law on February 1, 1968, he was minister of transport. But Hellyer's carefully laid succession plans came to naught. At the Liberal leadership convention he lost to newcomer Pierre Trudeau. In the words of Jack Granatstein, one of Canada's foremost military historians, Trudeau viewed soldiers as "unintelligent thugs." Under Trudeau, who became prime minister less than two months after unification came into effect, the downward spiral of the armed forces picked up speed.

Rumours abound that it was Trudeau, never a firm supporter of or believer in the military, who directed a name change from the Canadian Armed Forces to the less warlike-sounding Canadian Forces. Hellyer's ambitions drove him to jump to the Progressive Conservatives. When he lost his bid for leadership of that party, he later returned to the Liberals. Unable to win the leadership of either mainstream party, Hellyer created his own in 1997 and became its first leader. The Canadian Action Party has never won a seat.

## "SNIFFLE"

IN JANUARY 1968—the month before unification—NATO's Supreme Allied Commander Atlantic activated a new squadron consisting of half a dozen destroyer-type ships from different nations. The Standing Naval Force Atlantic, Stanavforlant in naval parlance, was abbreviated to SNFL, pronounced "sniffle" by sailors. Ships moved in and out of the

*Led by their flagship, the destroyer helicopter escort HMCS Annapolis, warships of NATO's multinational Standing Naval Force Atlantic exercise in the North Sea, June 26, 1974, (L–R) West German frigate FGS Augsberg, British frigate HMS Sirius, HMCS Annapolis, Dutch destroyer HNLMS Rotterdam, and American destroyer USS Julius A. Furer.*

squadron from various contributing nations on a rotational basis, as did its commander, who acted as the flotilla's commodore for a year at a time.

The squadron's raison d'être was multipurpose. It was continuously operational and worked on improving standard operating procedures between NATO nations, particularly in ASW. It showed allied solidarity to the rest of the world, especially the Warsaw Pact. It gave NATO an immediate-reaction naval force for emergencies, one around which a larger force could concentrate. It also provided the Supreme Allied Commander Atlantic with a force under his direct control for surveillance and monitoring of the Soviet fleet.

After initial reluctance to participate, based on a misunderstanding by the navy about committing vessels to SNFL on a permanent basis, Canada's first ship joined the squadron in 1970. Since then, there has always been a Canadian vessel in the squadron. Over the years, several Canadian warships have participated—usually for six months at a time— and Canadian commodores or rear admirals have been in command on a rotational basis. Canada's expertise in helicopter ASW operations quickly became recognized as among the very best among the contributing nations, despite its aging fleet. SNFL has visited Halifax on many occasions. Today, SNFL is known as Standing NATO Maritime Response Force Group 1 and is controlled by Allied Command Operations (formerly known as SHAPE— Supreme Headquarters Allied Powers Europe).

## A DIMINISHED FLEET

SINCE THE HEADY NEW-SHIP construction days of the 1950s and early 1960s, the navy has seen a steady decline in the number of its ships and—some would argue—in

*The operational support ship* HMCS Protecteur *replenishes a Tribal class destroyer helicopter escort at sea (right), in the company of* HMCS Annapolis *and a Sea King helicopter.*

its capabilities. Three operational support ships, known as AORs, to resupply the fleet over long distances were commissioned between 1963 and 1970. HMCS *Provider*, the first AOR, was the largest ship ever built for the navy in Canada. After yeoman service around the world, she was paid off in 1998. Using lessons learned from experience with *Provider*, the next two AORs, *Preserver* and *Protecteur*, were commissioned at Saint John, New Brunswick, in 1969 and 1970, respectively. They included several significant design changes. All three ships were built to carry three ASW helicopters as spares for the fleet. Unlike *Provider*, her later sisters are armed with a twin 3-inch gun. *Preserver* and *Protecteur* are long overdue for replacement, but the proposed acquisition of three joint support ships has made little headway in the face of competing requirements for defence dollars.

In 1989, the Canadian navy reached a postwar low: only thirteen major warships— most of them on their final legs—as well as three O-boats and three AORs. All twenty St. Laurent class destroyers and their successors in the Restigouche, Mackenzie, and Annapolis classes have since been decommissioned. Four much larger Iroquois class destroyers (*Iroquois, Athabaskan, Huron*, and *Algonquin*), also known as the Tribal class because they were named after First Nations tribes, were commissioned in 1972 and 1973. They carried two helicopters each and were armed with a 5-inch multipurpose gun, two triple-mount torpedo launchers, a Mark X anti-submarine mortar, and two four-round Sea Sparrow surface-to-air missile launchers for point anti-aircraft defence. The Tribals were the first ships in the world to be powered by gas turbine engines.

*The destroyer* HMCS *Iroquois, lead ship of her class, was commissioned in 1972.*

During the early 1990s, all four destroyers underwent the Tribal Update and Modernization Programme, known as TRUMP, to change them to area defence destroyers while maintaining some anti-submarine capabilities. Their main weapon now is the SM-2 long-range anti-aircraft missile. Installation of this system required the replacement of the 5-inch gun with a smaller but much faster firing 76-mm gun. A Phalanx 20-mm close-in weapons system was also added for self-defence.

## THE LAST CORVETTE

IN 1985, THE NAVY CELEBRATED its seventy-fifth anniversary. Highlights of the year were an international fleet review in Bedford Basin, which consisted of thirty-four warships from several nations, including eight frigates from SNFL. Among the ships in Bedford Basin was a newcomer, which—paradoxically—was the oldest ship there. On May 4, 1985, the actual anniversary date and the day before Battle of the Atlantic Sunday, *Sackville*, Canada's last surviving corvette of the 123 that served in the RCN during the Second World War, made her first official appearance after having been lovingly restored.

In any story about Halifax, the navy, and the Second World War, *Sackville's* tale forms a part. *Sackville* managed to be saved because she continued to be used after the war and operated as a research vessel at Halifax until 1982. As part of her restoration, *Sackville* was designated as Canada's National Naval Memorial and is maintained by a trust. Today she spends her fair-weather months alongside Sackville Landing next to the Maritime Museum of the Atlantic, where hundreds of thousands of visitors have toured the ship.

HMCS Sackville, *refurbished to her wartime glory, in Halifax Harbour, where she serves as Canada's National Naval Memorial.*

Despite the best efforts of the trust, *Sackville* continues to feel the effects of age—especially her hull—and deteriorates daily. Trust members hope that sometime in the near future she can be put on permanent display out of the water and inside a revitalized and expanded maritime museum.

## THE PERSIAN EXCURSION

IRONICALLY, THE END OF the Cold War marked the navy's first shooting war since Korea. Saddam Hussein's August 1990 invasion of Kuwait led to an immediate UN response, which included a naval task force under Commodore Ken Summers. Three weeks after the invasion, HMC Ships *Athabaskan*, *Terra Nova*, and *Protecteur* sailed from Halifax on Operation Friction—25 per cent of the country's operational warships carrying almost a thousand sailors, air personnel, and air defence artillery gunners. Modifications that would normally have taken eighteen months to complete were done in ten days of twenty-four-hour schedules in the Halifax dockyard. Fortunately, much of the required equipment was at hand, intended for the new Canadian Patrol Frigate shipbuilding programme.

The destroyer *Athabaskan* served as the flagship of the Canadian naval task group and required extensive and hurried modifications before she deployed. As she had not undergone TRUMP at the time, a Phalanx weapons system was added. Additional air defence protection was provided by shoulder-launched Javelin missiles, operated by gunners of the Royal Canadian Artillery. The older improved Restigouche class destroyer *Terra Nova* and the AOR *Protecteur* received several new systems as well. Between them, the three ships also carried five Sea King helicopters, which underwent extensive modifications.

It was only when the task force reached Italy that its mission was assigned: it would operate in the Persian Gulf as part of the Multinational Interception Force enforcing the UN trade embargo against Iraq. As the war had changed from a defensive to an offensive one, the role of the Canadian ships changed as well. Canada was put in charge of a newly created Combat Logistics Force. Its role was to keep the coalition naval forces in the gulf supplied with fuel, ammunition, and spare parts. Canada was chosen to lead it largely because of *Athabaskan*'s superior command and control capabilities, as well as the known professionalism of Canadian sailors and their familiarity with American methods.

Captain "Dusty" Miller, the task force chief of staff and second in command, was appointed Combat Logistics Force Co-ordinator in charge of the force, which consisted of ten escort and twenty replenishment ships from a dozen or so nations, plus up to forty-five helicopters. The force operated out of a thirty-seven by thirty-seven kilometre holding area, known as the Pachyderm Palace to the Canadians and the Ponderosa to

TOP HMCS Athabaskan *departing Halifax on Operation Friction, August 24, 1990.*
BOTTOM HMCS Protecteur *replenishes* HMC Ships Terra Nova *(left) and* Athabaskan *(right) on the way to the Persian Gulf during Operation Friction, September 1990.*

the Americans. Miller was the only non-American to hold such a high naval command during the war. After successfully playing its part in the liberation of Kuwait and the invasion of Iraq, the task force returned home to Halifax to a tumultuous welcome on April 7, 1991.

## NEW SHIPS

BUDGET CUTS DURING THE 1990s resulted in one of the four Tribals, *Huron*, being left without a crew. She was paid off in 2005 and sunk during a live-fire exercise on the West Coast by her sister ship *Algonquin* in 2007. The TRUMP was intended as a stopgap measure only, as the ships' radar systems are outdated. Although the Tribals were originally intended for decommissioning by 2010, there are no replacements on the horizon, and other improvements are expected to give the three remaining ships a few more years of service.

Between 1992 and 1996, the navy commissioned twelve City class frigates, known as the Canadian Patrol Frigate. Six are in the Halifax batch, while the other six are referred to as the Montreal batch. The construction of these warships was the largest and most complex project in Canadian military history. While the City class frigates were being commissioned, twelve multi-role smaller ships—the Kingston class maritime coastal defence vessels—entered service between 1995 and 1998. These ships are manned largely by long-term reserve callouts.

One of the most controversial Canadian ship-acquisition programmes in history was the replacement of Canada's Oberon class submarines. After toying briefly with the idea of acquiring a dozen nuclear-powered submarines in the 1980s, Canada purchased the entire RN Upholder class of submarines in 1998, although they had been laid up for five years. Known in Canadian service as the Victoria class, all four have been plagued with

*The modern Canadian fleet is based on twelve Canadian patrol frigates and three area defence destroyers, such as (L-R) HMC Ships* Vancouver, Toronto, *and* Iroquois.

*HMCS* Victoria *sails past Maugers Beach on McNabs Island.* Victoria *is the lead boat of four Upholder class submarines purchased from Britain.*

problems from the beginning. One of them, HMCS *Chicoutimi*, suffered a severe fire while transiting to Halifax in October 2004. Lieutenant Chris Saunders later died of smoke inhalation during an emergency evacuation flight. *Chicoutimi* will require several years of repairs before she is seaworthy.

## HELICOPTERS

WHEN CANADA PURCHASED FORTY-ONE Sikorsky Sea King helicopters in 1963 for ASW work they were top-of-the-line aircraft. In the navy's centennial year, twenty-eight remain in service, often referred to as ancient, geriatric, or venerable; indeed, they are. Those still flying are plagued by flameouts, engine stalls, generator failures, and gearbox problems. They are long overdue for replacement. The Conservative government of Brian Mulroney intended to buy new shipborne helicopters in the 1990s, during a time of drastic military cost-cutting, which coincided with the end of the Cold War.

Many Canadians opposed the purchase, looking for the so-called "peace dividend" that was supposed to accrue to the country as the decades-old East-West confrontation ended. But successive Canadian governments had already claimed the dividend before it came due, as reflected in the sad state of the CF in terms of manpower, equipment, and funding. In any case, the Tories went ahead and announced the purchase of fifty EH-101 top-line helicopters for $4.8 billion, to be known in Canadian service as the Cormorant. In the end,

*A Sea King helicopter dipping sonar, February 14, 1974.*

the Conservatives' plans came to naught.

During the 1993 election campaign, Liberal leader Jean Chrétien attacked the Tory plan as wasteful and termed the EH-101s as "Cadillacs," providing more than the navy actually needed. The Liberals won the election, and in one of Chrétien's first acts as prime minister he cancelled the deal. He trumpeted the nearly five hundred million dollars that Canada had to pay in cancellation fees as fiscal prudence, and the navy was still without a Sea King replacement.

During Chrétien's time in office, and that of his successor Paul Martin, pressure continued on the government to replace the Sea King. In 2004, more than a decade after the Conservatives announced the EH-101 purchase, the Liberals finally decided to spend $3.2 billion on the acquisition of twenty-eight Sikorsky S-92s, to be known in Canadian service as the Cyclone. Generally, the CF would have preferred the EH-101, but the Liberals were caught in a trap of their own making. In 1998, they had purchased fifteen Cormorants to replace the aging Labrador search and rescue helicopter. To now buy additional EH-101s would have repudiated their earlier cancellation and its attendant squandering of money, despite the fact that having one type of maritime helicopter would have made it far easier to train aircrew and technicians as well as maintain spare parts. The delivery schedule for the Cyclones has been amended several times from the original in-service date of 2008, and may not occur until sometime between 2012 and 2014.

## WOMEN IN THE NAVY

AFTER DENYING WRENS THE OPPORTUNITY to serve at sea for many years, the navy was gradually forced to accept women aboard its ships. Starting in the mid-1960s and continuing for several years, the position of women in the navy came under close scrutiny through a combination of internal and external influences. These included the 1965 Defence Minister's Manpower Study; the 1971 Royal Commission on the Status of Women; the 1978 Canadian Human Rights Act; the 1979–84 SWINTER (Service Women in Non-Traditional Environments and Roles) Trials; the 1982 Charter of Rights and

*Master Corporal Wilma Carroll stands watch aboard* HMCS Cormorant *while Leading Seaman Al Boudreau flashes a signal lamp during* SWINTER *Trials, September 25, 1980.*

Freedoms; and the CREW (Combat-Related Employment of Women) Trials of 1987–89. During this period, the integration and unification of the three separate services occurred on February 1, 1968. Women in the RCN were no longer WRCNS and, along with females in the other two services, they became full members of the new CF, without belonging to separate women's components.

The naval portion of the SWINTER Trials saw the first female sailors assigned to a naval vessel. Between 1980 and 1984, eight to thirteen females served aboard HMCS *Cormorant*, a non-combatant fleet diving tender based at Halifax and commanded by Lieutenant Commander Gil Morrison. At the end of the trial, the results showed that non-combatant ships could easily accommodate mixed-gender crews and that the women could effectively carry out their assigned tasks in them. The navy decided that females were suitable for postings to "minor war vessels, such as patrol boats, gate vessels, and small training vessels." For his part, Morrison had no time for those who objected to women aboard ships.

Three years after completion of the SWINTER Trials, the CREW Trials took place. These new trials were the direct result of recommendations made by the Parliamentary Subcommittee on Equality Rights, which urged that all CF trades and occupations be open to women. The subcommittee's decision was based on the Equality Rights section of the Canadian Charter of Rights and Freedoms, which came into effect in April 1985. In 1987, the navy began posting women into combat units as part of the trials but was overtaken by a ruling of the Canadian Human Rights Commission Tribunal in 1989. It directed that all navy trades be opened to females, with the exception of service in submarines due to extremely close quarters and limited living space. This new right to serve in all occupations brought with it a liability to serve anywhere. Interestingly, some senior naval service women resented the newly imposed liability to serve at sea.

The first women into the trades and occupations recently opened to them were not always happy with the public attention they garnered as "pioneers" or "ground-breakers." In *A History of Women in the Canadian Military*, Barbara Dundas recorded some of their opinions. As Ordinary Seaman Cheryl Whalen noted, "I don't want to be first at anything anymore, I just want to get on with my career." Her colleague, Leading Seaman Susan Gencarelli, a stoker, agreed: "I didn't want to be centred out for attention. I just wanted to be treated as an equal."

As more women enrolled in the navy and served at sea, the navy reconfigured mess-decks in its warships to provide accommodation for mixed-gender crews. This occasionally left women out of the loop. Gencarelli complained of being isolated from the male stokers' messdeck: "When the stokers get together, we're left out. We miss a lot because of that. When I was doing my training, I did a lot of it by myself because I just couldn't sit down in the messdeck and talk it out with the other stokers."

In 1999, the Minister's Advisory Board on Canadian Forces Gender Integration and

*The Sailors' Memorial in Halifax's Point Pleasant Park was unveiled in 1967, replacing an earlier one on the slopes of Citadel Hill. It reads "In honour of those men and women of the navy, army and merchant marine of Canada whose names are inscribed here. Their graves are unknown but their memory shall endure." The memorial lists 3,119 names.*

Employment Equity, a group established in 1990 to report on the progress of female integration, recommended that Maritime Command "remove all restrictions and barriers to the service of women in submarines." This recommendation was driven in large part by the acquisition of the Victoria class submarines, which provided much more spacious living areas than their predecessors, the O-boats.

The next year, the Commander of Maritime Command announced that women could serve in submarines. This was followed in 2003 by the first women to qualify for submarine service, when two female master seamen passed the submarine course conducted at Halifax. To date, six women have served in submarines, in combat information operator, sonar operator, communicator, and cook classifications. Further achievements by women in the navy included the first female flag officer in 1988 (Commodore Laraine Orthlieb, senior Naval Reserve advisor); the first ship's captain in 2003 (Lieutenant Commander Marta Mulkins, HMCS *Kingston*); the first female commander of a naval formation in 2007 (Commodore Jennifer Bennett, Naval Reserve); and the first female captain of a major warship in 2009 (Commander Josée Kurtz, HMCS *Halifax*).

## "DE-UNIFICATION?"

IN 1985, THE CONSERVATIVE GOVERNMENT fulfilled an election promise by putting the three separate services back into distinctive uniforms. But they did nothing more to reverse unification, including single service rank badges and titles (although the navy had previously succeeded in reinstating its traditional rank designations). The Conservatives should have gone further and "de-unified" the CF. The armed forces are quite capable of working together and conducting joint operations without being unified.

Throughout the disastrous unification process of the late 1960s, Paul Hellyer maintained the rest of the world was watching Canada closely and other countries would emulate his reorganization. Canadians—and the navy—are still waiting. It is unfortunate that the federal government did not use the navy's centennial year of 2010 as a fitting occasion to at least reinstate the three separate services with their proper, historical names—Royal Canadian Navy, Canadian Army, and Royal Canadian Air Force—an act that could have easily occurred with the stroke of a pen.

Despite the injustices inflicted on the navy over the years by a succession of unrealistic, uninformed, and uncaring governments, politicians, bureaucrats, and, to a certain extent, ordinary citizens, Canada's sailors have always risen to the occasion. They have willingly undertaken whatever their nation and its people have asked of them. They have been doing it for a hundred years; they will still be doing it a hundred years from now—and Halifax will continue to be their major home port.

# BIBLIOGRAPHY

Armstrong, John Griffith. *The Halifax Explosion and the Royal Canadian Navy: Inquiry and Intrigue*. Vancouver: University of British Columbia Press, 2002.

Banister, Lisa, ed. *Equal to the Challenge: An Anthology of Women's Experiences During World War II*. Ottawa: DND, 2001.

Barris, Ted. *Deadlock in Korea: Canadians at War, 1950–1953*. Toronto: Macmillan, 1999.

Boileau, John. *Fastest in the World: The Saga of Canada's Revolutionary Hydrofoils*. Halifax: Formac, 2004.

———. *Valiant Hearts: Atlantic Canada and the Victoria Cross*. Halifax: Nimbus, 2005.

———. *Historic Eastern Passage*. Halifax: Nimbus, 2007.

———. *Where the Water Meets the Land: The Story of the Halifax Harbour Waterfront*. Halifax: Saltscapes, 2007.

Boutilier, James A., ed. *RCN in Retrospect, 1910–1968*. Vancouver: University of British Columbia Press, 1982.

Darlington, Capt. Robert A. and Cdr. Fraser M. McKee. *The Canadian Naval Chronicle 1939–1945: The Successes and Losses of the Canadian Navy in World War II*. Revised edition. St. Catharines, Ont: Vanwell, 1998.

Dundas, Barbara. *A History of Women in the Canadian Military*. Montreal: Art Global, 2000.

Ferguson, Julie H. *Through a Canadian Periscope: The Story of the Canadian Submarine Service*. Toronto: Dundurn, 1995.

German, Cdr. Tony. *The Sea is at Our Gates: The History of the Canadian Navy*. Toronto: McClelland & Stewart, 1990.

Greer, Rosamond "Fiddy." *The Girls of the King's Navy*. Victoria: Sono Nis, 1983.

Hadley, Michael L. *U-Boats against Canada: German Submarines in Canadian Waters*. Montreal and Kingston: McGill-Queen's University Press, 1985.

Hadley, Michael L. and Roger Sarty. *Tin-Pots & Pirate Ships: Canadian Naval Forces & German Sea Raiders 1880–1918*. Montreal and Kingston: McGill-Queen's University Press, 1991.

Harding, Marguerite. *Through the Gates*. Bridgewater, NS: H and B Langille, 1999.

Irvine, Thomas A. *The Ice was all Between: The Circumnavigation of the North American Continent by HMCS Labrador in 1954*. New York: Longmans, Green, 1959.

Jensen, Latham B. *Tin Hats, Oilskins & Seaboots: A Naval Journey, 1938–1945*. Toronto: Robin Brass, 2000.

Kealy, J. D. F and E. C. Russell. *A History of Canadian Naval Aviation 1918–1962*. Ottawa: Queen's Printer, 1965.

Kimber, Stephen. *Sailors, Slackers and Blind Pigs: Halifax at War*. Toronto: Doubleday, 2002.

Lawrence, Hal. *A Bloody War: One Man's Memories of the Canadian Navy 1939–1945*. Toronto: Macmillan, 1979.

———. *Tales of the North Atlantic*. Toronto: McClelland & Stewart, 1985.

Macpherson, Ken and Ron Barrie. *The Ships of Canada's Naval Forces 1910–2002*. St. Catharines, Ont: Vanwell, 2002.

McClearn, Sandy. "HMCS *Kootenay* Gearbox Explosion." *The Canadian Navy of Yesterday and Today. http://www.hazegray.org/navhist/canada/postwar/restigou/ kootenay-explosion/*

McNeil, Bill. *Voices of a War Remembered: An Oral History of Canadians in World War II*. Toronto: Doubleday, 1991.

Melady, John. *Korea: Canada's Forgotten War*. Toronto: Macmillan, 1983.

Metson, Graham. *An East Coast Port...Halifax at War 1939–1945*. Toronto: McGraw-Hill Ryerson, 1981.

Meyers, Edward C. *Thunder in the Morning Calm: The Royal Canadian Navy in Korea 1950–1955*. St. Catharines, Ont: Vanwell, 1992.

Miller, Commodore Duncan (Dusty) and Sharon Hobson. *The Persian Excursion: The Canadian Navy in the Gulf War*. Clementsport, NS, and Toronto: Canadian Peacekeeping Press and Canadian Institute of Strategic Studies, 1995.

Milner, Marc. *Canada's Navy: The First Century*. Toronto: University of Toronto Press, 1999.

———, ed. *Canadian Military History: Selected Readings*. Toronto: Copp Clark Pitman, 1993.

Naftel, William D. *Halifax at War: Searchlights, Squadrons and Submarines 1939–1945*. Halifax: Formac, 2008.

Naval Officers' Association of Canada, Ottawa Branch. *Did We Say All? Salty Dips Vol. 3*. Ottawa: Love Printing, 1988.

Perkins, J. David. *The Canadian Submarine Service in Review*. St. Catharines, Ont: Vanwell, 2000.

Raddall, Thomas H. *Halifax: Warden of the North*. Halifax: Nimbus, 1993.

Smith, Marilyn Gurney. *The King's Yard: An Illustrated History of the Halifax Dockyard*. Halifax: Nimbus, 1985.

Robinson, Lt. N. David, ed. *Her Majesty's Canadian Ship Scotian, 1947–1997, Fiftieth Anniversary Souvenir Programme*. Halifax: Dalhousie Print Centre, 1997.

Soward, Stuart E. *Hands to Flying Stations: A Recollective History of Canadian Naval Aviation*, Vol. I: *1945–1954*, Vol. II: *1955–1969*. Victoria: Neptune Developments, 1993 and 1995.

Thorgrimsson, Thor and E. C. Russell. *Canadian Naval Operations in Korean Waters 1950–1955*. Ottawa: Queen's Printer, 1965.

Tucker, Gilbert Norman. *The Naval Service of Canada*, Vol. II: *Activities on Shore during the Second World War*. Ottawa: King's Printer, 1952.

Wright, H. Millard. *The Other Halifax Explosion: Bedford Magazine July 18–20, 1945*. Halifax: 2001.

# IMAGE CREDITS

# INDEX

Murray, Rear Admiral Leonard, 101–103, *102*, 105, 106, 108–109, *108. See also* V-E Day riots

Musée Maritime du Québec, 182

Musgrave, Cadet Alured, 12

*Musquash*, 27

Musquodoboit, Nova Scotia, 142

Myrhaugen, Colonel Lee, 159

**N**

*Nabob*, HMCS, 140

*Nanoose*, HMCS. *See Nootka*, HMCS

National Defence Headquarters, 110, 148, 184

National Harbours Board, 88, 164

National Research Council, 169

North Atlantic Treaty Organization (NATO), 148, 151, 182, 185–186

Naval Board, 123, 155, 162

Naval Control Service (NCS), 13, 56–58, *57, 58,* 59, 87. *See also* Oland, Commander Dick

Naval Headquarters, 173

Naval Officers' Association of Canada, 87

Naval Reserve Division, 43, 163

Naval Service Act, 1, 10

Naval Service of Canada, 10, 11

Navy League building, 44

Nelson Barracks, 97

Newcombe, Commander Edward, 22

Newfoundland, 29, 39, 52, 68, 122, 162

Newfoundland Escort Force, 46

*New Waterford*, HMCS, *161*

New York, New York, 15, 17, 70, 122

*Niobe*, HMCS, 1, *2,* 11–12, *12,* 16, 17, *17,* 25–29, *27, 28,* 36, 40

*Nipigon*, HMCS, 155

Nixon, Commander Edward, 12, 14

Noade, Stoker Jimmy, 72

*Nootka*, HMCS, 48, *125,* 126, 127–130, *127, 128, 130, 132, 159*

Norfolk, Virginia, 159, 160, 182

North America and West Indies Station, 18, 22

North American Aerospace Defence Command (NO-RAD), 146

North End Services Canteen, *97*

North Korea. *See under* Korean War

North Pole, 172, 175

North Sea, 6

Northwest Arm, 98, 150

Northwest Passage, 170, 175. *See also* Arctic; *Labrador*, HMCS

Norton, Commander Neil, 165, 168

**O**

*Oakville*, HMCS, 63–66

Oberon class submarine (O-boat), 152, *153,* 192, 198. *See also individual boat names*

O-boat. *See* Oberon class

O'Hara, Ordinary Seaman Ian, 73

*Ojibwa*, HMCS, 152

*Okanagan*, HMCS, 152

Oland, Colonel Sidney, 105

Oland, Commander Dick, *13,* 56–60, *59. See also* Naval Control Service

Olander, Captain Sven, 63

Oland, Victor, 59

*Onondaga*, HMCS, 152

*Ontario*, HMCS, 145

Operation Friction, 190

Operation Paukenschlag ("Drumbeat"), 53

Operation Scuppered, 150

Operation Squeegee, 129

Order of the British Empire, 136

Orpheus Theatre, *95*

Orthlieb, Commodore Laraine, 198

Ottawa (federal government), 22, 58, 162, 176

*Ottawa*, HMCS, 47, 155, 156. *See also Crusader*, HMS

Ottawa, Ontario, 112, 119

*Otter*, HMCS, 70–73, *71*

**P**

Pachyderm Palace, 190

Pacific, 6, 14, 140

Pacific Destroyer Division, 126

Padgett, Wren F. A., *118*

Palmer, Midshipman William, 14, 15

Panama Canal, 150, 174

Parliamentary Subcommittee on Equality Rights, 196

Patey, Vice Admiral Sir George, 22

*Patrician*, HMCS, 42, 44

*Patriot*, HMCS, 40, *41,* 42, 44, 176, *177*

Patrol Vessel, Whaler Type, 53

Payzant, Pete, 179

Pearson, Lester B. ("Mike"), 146, 184, 185

Peggy's Cove, Nova Scotia, 32

Pelletier, Germaine, 100

*Peregrine*, HMCS, 97

Perkins, J. David, 151

Persian Gulf, 190

Phalanx weapons system, 189, 190

Phipps Hornby, Rear Admiral R. S., 18, *18*

Piasecki HUP-3 helicopter, *174*

Plymouth, England, 147, 162, 165, 168